NEW RENAISSANCE

MAURICE ASH

# New Renaissance

*Essays in Search of Wholeness*

GREEN BOOKS

© Maurice Ash, 1987

First published by
Green Books
Hartland
Bideford
Devon EX39 6EE

*Illustrations:* Anthony Colbert
*Cover:* John Lane

British Library Cataloguing in Publication Data
Ash, Maurice
New Renaissance: In search of wholeness
1. Holism
I. Title
160 B818
ISBN 0 87009 800 5

Typeset by KMA Typesetting
70 The Square, Hartland
Printed by Hartnoll Bound
Victoria Square, Bodmin, Cornwall

to Ruth, and her spirit

# Contents

# *Preface*

This book, though it is actually a collection of articles and talks, sets out a position on a whole variety of issues in public or quasi-public life towards which I have had some responsibility over the past two decades. This position has had a certain consistency to it: enough, perhaps, to justify a book that could never otherwise have been written—and perhaps never should have been, as such, aside from one's everyday experiences.

The papers are either articles from *Town and Country Planning*, or *Resurgence*, or for The Green Alliance—all of which are thanked for their rights of reproduction—or talks, many of them given in my position as Chairman of The Dartington Hall Trust, a complex of industrial, commercial, agricultural, educational, artistic and research activities, all in the context of a rural estate. My especial thanks go to Satish Kumar, editor of *Resurgence*, who has encouraged the making of this book and is largely responsible for the selection and ordering of its material. It would, however, seem pointless to specify the origins of each piece, partly because the details are too numerous to mention, but also because it is in the nature of my position to treat as much of the context as of the particulars of each case. Nevertheless, perhaps the reader's indulgence should be asked if a certain repetitiveness ensues. My long-suffering audience has been varied, and a continuous flow of originality is not a necessary prerogative of a dissident against the ruling cast of mind, such as I seem to have been.

Maurice Ash
August, 1986

# Foreword

Readers who expect this book to be about one subject—say education—will be surprised to find that it is also about town and country planning, about economics, about the bewitchment of language. It is also 'about' nuclear power, Zen Buddhism and Islam.

It is exactly because of such habitual expectations that people are specialists and books have one subject—that we are in need of *New Renaissance*. It smashes the mind-set. It looks at things as they are and as a whole. In it, the world of affairs and the world of thought, of philosophy if you like, are interfused.

Thought, of course, is viewed with suspicion and philosophy is a dirty word. Thinkers do not act (they dream); workers do not think—particularly, that is, if they work with their hands. Here is a divide, a fundamental cleavage, one of many, between material and spiritual, between body and mind, between God and Caesar, between God and man expecially, at the very base of our current understanding. This chasm at the root of being Maurice Ash rejects. It is directly antithetical to his view of life, his ontology, as one of harmonic, organic oneness at the core of all being and of true human awareness. It is contrary to his sense of wholeness which includes both what he knows and what cannot be known.

In point of fact he knows a great deal. He was born in India, son of a working engineer. After school—at Greshams Holt in Norfolk—he took a degree in Economics at the London School of Economics; a fact expressed by his abiding (but to my taste wasteful) enthusiasm for *The Economist* which nestles alongside *Farmers Weekly*, Buddhist texts and books on or by Wittgenstein on his chair-side table. Even here, philosophy, metaphysics and practical affairs are not divorced, but seen as one.

After University, Maurice Ash's life took on an almost Castiglione-like largesse. He has been (and in some cases still is) a farmer, a publisher, a restauranteur, a sportsman, a father and, in the public realms, a man of many parts: Chairman of the Executive Committee of the Town and Country Planning Association, of the Green Alliance and , for twelve industrious years, of the Dartington Hall Trust, wherein he was involved in and responsible for a wide variety of human endeavours—farming again; forestry, gardening, the arts, education, research, welfare, community affaris. At the same time he has been supportive—and sometimes actively involved in—the activities of the Schumacher Society, the Yarner Trust, the Henry Moore Foundation and the Sharpham Trust which, with his late wife, Ruth's, encouragement, is the beneficiary of their estate in South Devon.

An abundant richness of experience, unusual in its variety, informs this miscellany of papers (written at different times for different readerships) with an exceptional strength and unity; the unity of understanding of (to adopt Wolfram von Eschenbach's description of Parzival) 'a brave man slowly wise.' Yet, if one imagines that the musings of a seventy year old 'philosopher-king' are hardly likely to disturb the even tenor of our ways; I urge you to think again.

*New Renaissance* is dynamite; a book of exceptional boldness and originality, at once articulating what we have always known to be true and questioning the very foundations of the Christian and Greek rationalist traditions.

Christian theism and Cartesian subject-object dualism have been equally, and disastrously, divisive and Maurice Ash is not afraid to tell us so. He is the child in The Emperor's New Clothing telling us of our religious predicament, of our spiritual vacuity, of our minds and hearts torn by divisions but—as yet—barely ready to face the rigours of non-duality, of mindfulness. *New Renaissance* is not, however, as its title suggests, a despondent book—on the contrary it proclaims a new springtime, a new cogito: the essential basis for a new civilization informed by meaning—and hence with the spirit. On the seeming chaos on whose verge we stand today it offers not merely hope but ideas, unity, reconciliation and the expression of love.

'There are', Maurice Ash writes, 'mysterious under-currents at work today. As animals know about the approaching storm before we do, or birds fly up before an earthquake, so people are fashioning a new way of life'. It is this way of life, non-idealistic, non-dualistic, playful, holy, the *New Renaissance* envisions. It is my belief that the following pages will contribute to its realization.

John Lane
September 1986

# CHAPTER ONE

# *The New Renaissance*

# The New Renaissance

A few years ago I asked a leading authority on Wittgenstein if the latter's thought had had any impact on our society or culture. He considered the question for a moment, then, looking at me quizzically, 'No', he said, 'Why? Do you think it should?' The response left me nonplussed, and we lapsed into pleasantries. Privately, I thought, alas! for the ivory tower of modern philosophy—and yet I remained, over the years, fascinated by Wittgenstein's work. I should add that, in an afterthought, my philosopher friend hazarded that perhaps Wittgenstein had had some influence upon the social sciences. In this I'm sure he had in mind Peter Winch's *The Idea of a Social Science*, which as long ago as 1958 had, almost casually, dropped a seed of doubt from which the rot in the self-confidence of social scientists as intellectual followers of the natural scientists could arguably be dated. Yet, with the years, I've come to realize that my friend perhaps spoke from a deeper wisdom, and that the one qualification he made to what he said was all the more extraordinary in that Wittgenstein himself—beyond the tragic reference in the opening of his posthumous *Philosophical Investigations* to 'the darkness of these times'—referred but little to the condition of society.

The deeper wisdom of my professor friend pertained, I suspect, to Wittgenstein's own comment that 'philosophy leaves everything as it is'. This comment had grown out of his disillusionment with the absolutes, the verbal constructs, of Western thought. Any resonances aside for the cognoscenti of Godel's Theorem, the statement in question was all of a piece with that other remark: 'The purpose of philosophy is to show the fly the way out of the flybottle'. The purpose is, that is to say, to dispel the illusions that words generate in us, but not to define the Good, the True or the Beautiful. However, if this is so, there must be behind philosophy an idea of how the world is when it is not damaged by our abuse of words. In brief, then, this idea must be that the world is holy; it is as it is. All that we call 'history' is the tale of our bewitchment by language to make things seem to be where nothing is. The only discovery philosophy has to make is to know when to be able to stop doing it: which is tantamount, it seems to me, to an act of worship—or, at the very least, to a therapy.

What matters in all this is not any arcane philosophical discussion, but a recognition that we have here the groundings of Western non-dualistic thought. Wittgenstein had himself said in conversation with his great contemporary, G. E. Moore, that there seemed to be a 'kink' developing in Western thought, comparable to Galileo's invention of dynamics. And, of course, we now recognize that the centrality of Certainty in our mind-set has been displaced by Nature's inherent indeterminancy, and that the detachment of observer from observed is a fiction, and so forth. The art of Henry Moore, to take but one example (if 'art' is still the word), makes but little sense if not seen in this context: and Beckett, surely, also—presages, both.

Wittgenstein's own journey in search of our logically irreducible absolutes had begun from the seemingly ineluctible premises of dualistic thought—of a mind which understands the facts about the world that words describe— but was to result, when the hopelessness of that search became evident, in the repudiation of the very work, the *Tractatus*, for which his contemporaries held him in awe. (His loathing for those who associated him—and still inexcusable do—with the Logical Positivists may serve to mark the fixity of the mind-set against which he henceforth contended.) The outcome, though it is called 'ordinary language philosophy,' was not an alternative theory: precisely not. It was, rather, an inexhaustible series of instances—a 'deliberate unphilosophy', as a critic has complained—of the disillusions to which we are prone by reason of our bewitchment by language and the reifications to which it leads us. Nor is it surprising that Wittgenstein's renown in his lifetime held echoes of a return to the verbal tradition, for Socrates himself had warned of the dangers of our seduction by the permanence of the written word. (In Zen: 'If you meet the Buddha on the way, kill him!') Wittgenstein's product, at all events, was not even a 'book', with a beginning, a middle and an end. And, such as it was, it stemmed from the 'great inversion' he was forced to make to escape from the mind-body duality that had first led him down his blind alley, and which has held Western civilization—both in its triumphant exploitation of the earth, and in its own inexorable disintegration—so long in thrall.

The great inversion in question refers to the presumption that words picture reality. Suppose, rather, and to use the licence of an aphorism, we do not say what we know: we know what we say? For instance (and it is an instance some critics find indigestible), perhaps we do not learn the meaning of the past by connecting it, as children, with our thought in the past, but rather only by acquiring the language of the past tense: 'the meaning of a word is its use in the language'. More acceptably, perhaps, words and the world are inextricably entwined. This, then, bespeaks a non-dualism—and therewith a rejection of the innate superiority of the human mind—which is not merely to discard the competing monisms of idealism and materialism by which our culture has perennially been ravaged, but is no longer to take as given the subject-object structure of all our grammar. It is, surely, the most far-reaching of themes imaginable.

Nevertheless, whilst it may be the case that philosophy (true wisdom) leaves everything as it is, yet the fictions of our grammar itself are to be rejected. We have contrived a world, in fact, in which 'philosophy' has reified experience, whether of Nature or society, to fabricate structures that are only fictionalized projections of our private worlds. We have made 'the economy' out of our house-keeping, the Nation State out of our community life, 'classes' out of our social relationships, a whole bewilderment of regulations structuring our lives, as permanent as any high stone walls, to say nothing of ideological tyrannies. However, the rejection of these fictions is ultimately not a matter of linguistic philosophy, but of how we live. There is a huge task of de-institutionalization confronting Western civilization.

Yet the key-stone of this arch of institutions is the Judeo-Christian fixation on the 'I'—its sins, guilt and salvation—which is the ego-centric *fons et origo* of Western philosophy and its death-wracked society. This is the fixation which makes us so vulnerable to the bewitchment of language, whereby we have come to lock ourselves into unnumerable boxes, each separate from the other, until all sense of meaning of one in terms of another has been lost. These boxes, these specialisms, are separate because in dualistic thought mind and body are separate, alien substances. Of course, Descartes understood that this logical void must somehow be filled. 'God would not deceive us,' he said of it, thus making of God a necessary function of dualism: a reification to which we are obliged to subscribe. Like all reifications, however, this too has served its time and has been dispensed with by the arrogance of Humanism. And so we are left with the present vacuum of meaningless knowledge. No wonder things fall apart! Whilst, therefore, the changes in the grammar of life will have to be lived—and they will involve more than motor-cycle maintenance, though there will be that too—they will only be cosmetic so long as we cling to this fatal core of our culture.

How, then, is there to be a breakdown in our rigid compartments of dialogue? How is the baker to relate to the candlestick maker—or the computer operator—so that his bread shall recover its savour? It is a question, surely, of the spirit that infuses our language. For its spirit is part of any grammar. The meanings we convey can depend upon a smile or a scowl, upon a pervasive sense of optimism or despair, upon gestures of animation or despondence. The spirit is the governing relationship of language, connecting the knower to the known. And, given the discrete nature of language—its separation into words—the spirit that informs it can give less or more coherence to the manifold forms that life is bound to take. If we suffer today from a spiritual deprivation it is because reductionistic thought has ensured that nothing connects any more.

Happily the spirit is abroad that would speak a language of wholeness rather than of parts. It goes under the description of Green thinking and, with an increasingly confident disregard of the old logic, it challenges the conventional wisdom of our ways. It has the temerity to ignore the abstractions by which we vainly compound the complexities we seek to escape. It does this largely intuitively—and by ridicule of the conventions. The danger in this, however, is that it can lapse into mere romanticism, the sub-culture of our ruling rationalism: like, say, the defence of the privileges of Green Belts, when the need is for the creation of a whole new landscape. When one looks, for instance, at the social geography of Britain—at the squalid cities, the incohate suburbs, the empty countryside (that still living testament to the Deserted Village and monument to the Enclosures, but so appealing to the unquiet urban mind in its detachment and remoteness)—one is aware of the tinder-dry potential for a flowering of compassionate human energy. It is this suppressed energy that puts one in mind of a new Renaissance.

Yet it should not be thought that this new Renaissance might be any repetition of the old. Certainly, it concerns an overturning of the old Knowledge, but it is not any new individualism that is in view. On the contrary, the ego-centric philosophy of the West is what lies in the discard. The core of any new Renaissance, rather—and the rationale without which it risks being prey to the apocalyptic and millenarian eccentricities of the times, to say nothing of false dawns in the arts, when the arts have become the stereotype of stereotypes—is to be found in non-dualism. In the West, meditation is probably as near as we have come to the mode of non-dualistic thought. This, however, is largely a copying of Eastern forms. What Wittgenstein showed in his lonely, titanic struggle was that in the West the ground is found for our own evolution of non-dualism.

We can be sure that the old Renaissance did not develop simply because the forms of Classical culture became available to be copied. There must, for whatever reason, have been a readiness to adopt these models. This is where any analogy with a new Renaissance becomes valid. Eastern religious texts have been available as curiosities for perhaps two hundred years. Schopenauer's thinking was touched by them—and Schopenauer was one of the few philosophers to interest Wittgenstein. But it is only with the self-evident sterility of Western dualism, accompanied by the erosion of the barrier in that thought between theology and philosophy, that the flood-gates are being opened to the far richer and more subtle textures of Eastern philosophy. This has been dramatically demonstrated by the testimony of the American scholar, Robert Thurman (*Tsong Khapa's Speech of Gold*), who has said that the great texts of the Tibetan school, arguably the liveliest of the ancient traditions, would not even have been translatable, let alone intelligible to him, had it not been for his awareness of Wittgenstein's thought. Chris Gudmunsen (*Wittgenstein and Buddhism:* reprinting) has likewise drawn attention to the astounding parallels between Wittgenstein's rejection of Russell's atomism and the Mahayanan supersession of the Abidharmists (those who counted on individual enlightenment alone) some two thousand years ago. And there are others. So a treasury has been unlocked and is waiting for us to profit from it.

But a word of warning is in order. The prognosis is not of a glorious future for Western civilization in receipt of one of those shots in the arm—like the Crusades, or the Inquisition, or the conquest of the New World, or the Industrial Revolution—upon which, for reasons I forebear to speculate upon, its renewal seems ever-dependent. (Yet remember! Columbus was sent home from his third voyage mad and in chains. Why did it come to that?) Our culture is assuredly very sick, and the parallels with Rome's long drawn out agony are frightening in their comparable weariness of the spirit. 'Yesterday a drop of semen, tomorrow a handful of spice and ashes,' wrote the Emperor Marcus Aurelius towards the end of the second century, AD 'In the life of man, his time is but a moment, his being an incessant flux, his senses a dim rushlight, his body a prey of worms, his soul an unquiet eddy, his fortune dark, his fame doubtful. In short, all that is of the body is as coursing waters, all that is of the soul as dreams and vapours. An empty pageant, a stage play; flocks of sheep; herds of cattle; a tussle of spearmen; a bone flung among a pack of curs; a crumb tossed into a pond of fish; ants loaded and labouring; mice scared and scampering; puppets jerking on their strings—that is life.' He speaks for us yet, we of this century of the Holocaust, of Hiroshima, of the bone of a weekly wage and of the drug epidemic. Some hundred years later Constantine was to call upon the Christians to defend the corrupted city, whose own gods had fallen into ridicule— and so Authority was set on a new course.

That course having now been run, however, to the defence of what Eternal City should we in our own times turn? Hopefully, to no such illusion, nor even to the gentler tyranny of some New Jerusalem! These are just the kind of spells under which we fall when language 'goes on holiday'. When language ceases its task of simply illuminating our condition, that is, and seeks rather to fabricate it, when it loses its roots in poetry, in one way or another it encages us.

So by now, we have been endowed with the wisdom, if we wish to use it, to prevent our falling into the same error. It is perhaps even dangerously rhetorical, despite the quite fundamental transformation afoot, to speak in terms of a new 'Renaissance'. After all, at the time of the Renaissance itself nobody presumably thought of themselves as living through such a period: they took life as it came, and were only retrospectively fossilized by their followers. Moreover, as when a tide flows in it first fills the isolated runnels and the rock pools before it swells across the estuary, we are only at the early stage of recognition of the change. Yet, for instance, the reversal of two hundred years of rural depopulation, which the last Census revealed, is not to be explained away by any statistical sleight-of-hand, nor does it equate with any significant increase in material prosperity in rural areas—and certainly not in their provision of public services. The presumption must be, rather, that people want to escape from the anomie of urban life, perhaps even because of the provisions it makes, because a major shift in values is occurring.

Cities, in fact, together with the mentality that sustains them, are being rendered obsolete by networks of electronic communications. A multitude of small initiatives is replacing the grandiose formulae of yesterday. But what is so interesting about smallness is that it is hailed as 'beautiful'. Therein lies a veritable sea-change. For, when the aesthetic takes primacy over the moral, we can be sure that the separation of self from the world, which is the prerequisite of any concern for moral behaviour, is giving way to a sense of wholeness, to patterns of living in which self and world are indivisible. This is to go beyond any notion of stewardship of the environment, for the environment is not ours to be stewards of.

Lastly, then, wholeness is necessary, but it is not sufficient. Without spirit wholeness may be empty, a mere sum of parts: or worse, malign, as the totalitarian experience has shown. What wholeness does, which reductionism cannot do, is to confront us with the grammar of the language of the spirit. Yet the evidence grows that the soil has been prepared. Not only in Britain, but throughout Western Europe, people are responding less and less to hypnosis by the quantified allurements of the Industrial Era, and in a swelling flood are realizing Ruskin's dictum that 'there is no wealth but life'.

CHAPTER TWO

# The Politics
# of Wholeness

# The Politics of Wholeness

## The New Paradigm

Now thrive the ideologues. In their tents the opposing armies sharpen their logic. The populace itself seeks shelter where it can between these camps, its political world threatened and its disdain for all politicians almost absolute. Though some speak of reforming a system ever more precariously balanced, by making new alliances within it, few people in the pits of their stomachs believe that any combination of the old political forces could work. For the climate of life is deeply unsettled and changes are upon it that bring all our political certainties into question.

My thesis is, indeed, that we have reached our present constitutional crisis precisely because we have been driven by certainty. The last and fittest survivors of our political world are the ideologues, each proclaiming their contrary certitudes. To make this case, however, one must look beneath even the major eruptions of these times; beneath inflation, structural unemployment and de-industrialization; beneath the exhaustion of the earth's resources and the pollution of our nest, the earth; beneath even resurgent Islam and waning Christianity; beneath the desperate gamble with nuclear power; beneath the death of our cities; and beneath the balance of terror upon which civilisation and perhaps life itself, now depends. All these, and more, are the daily preoccupations of our bewildered politicians, who try to fit their received ideologies to such a world and, if they are men of candour, shrink back. Politics as we know it can no longer deal with these issues because it shares the very mentality out of which they arose.

To argue this position I must discuss the shift of paradigm which alone can illuminate what is happening. By this I mean the change in the pattern of our thought, in the template of our minds: of the analogues by which we form the facets of our lives. Plato's Greece marked one such moment of change, with the establishment of idealistic thought; Christianity signalled another, with mankind partaking of the divine; and Copernicus heralded another, with the earth no longer the centre of the Universe, but a speck in the abyss. We find ourselves at as great a moment of change.

In this context, then, I want to contend that we are passing from the Age of Knowledge, which has held sway these last four hundred years or so, to an Age of Meaning; from the Enlightenment and the counter-Enlightenment (Romanticism), to what can so far only be called the Alternative Movement. In so doing I shall need to speak of the flaws of reductionism and the quantitative method: of the different kinds of knowledge there are: of language and uncertainty: of the emergent primacy of form and process: of the strange promise of the future, and much else that may seem politically abstruse. But I shall hope to relate the significance of 'Green' politics—the politics of a new springtime—to all this. I would only ask that the magnitude of the shift of paradigm might be entertained. The growing evidence of events, after all, suggests what is afoot.

## The Politics of Knowledge

The paradigm within which we now live—and I would say endure, and whose consequences become increasingly insufferable—is that of knowledge. Knowledge itself is power, in Bacon's dictum; and power is the stuff of politics. We think of the epoch which Bacon announced as the Enlightenment. The fact that it consisted of two parallel streams—rational idealism and scientific empiricism—is relatively unimportant. The arbitrary power of princes and the obscuranticism of the Church provided their common ground and the Enlightenment as a whole set out the field of a new politics: the politics of the power of knowledge.

Descartes was the Apostle of the rational. He contrasted the thinking Self, as an indubitable reality, with the world from which it was separate and which was governed by the detectable laws of number of its particles. He thus staked out a territory for those who might possess this new certainty, the purpose of which, as he announced in *The Method*, was to make men the Lords and Masters of Nature.

Of course, science is not to be confused with Cartesianism. It is empirical, rather, proceeding from observed knowledge of the particular, not from any premise about the whole Universe. Science itself at first relied upon the Church to take care of a universal Providence. But, like any worldly authority, the Church was riven; it was a rift which was to drive Newton himself—for whom Descartes' views of the inanimacy of Nature were blasphemous—for a whole decade into a secret, hopeless and, through mercury poisoning, nearly fatal pursuit of alchemy. It was the certainty in itself which scientific observation offered that perforce filled this void of lost meaning. The reductionism of science was thus sanctified as our myth.

The bent of the Judaeo-Christian mind to find an answer to the religious question—the question, why is there anything at all?—in terms of one Creator of all the things there are, was satisfied by the merging of these two streams of the Enlightenment into a marvellous aesthetic of the universe as a perfect machine, set in motion by the Prime Mover. The clock was the symbol for the paradigm of knowledge. Alexander Pope's rythms reflected it, and Jefferson's Declaration of

Independence was its supreme political expression. Man, made as he was by the Great Architect—as a moral being, and therefore created equal, separate from the beasts—was in pursuit of his natural rights, which were to the social universe as gravity was to the natural, and which would be found in an harmonious social contract, complete with all its working parts. Happiness itself could be quantified by the greatest good of the greatest number. The politics of the democracies, indeed, as an inter-action of atomistic individuals, were fused in the paradigm of knowledge and thus in the mechanistic image. How sad it is, then, that today the machinery of state grinds to a halt, as happiness is translated into the arcane language of macro-economics and wage-bargaining!

Nevertheless, it is a danger for the Alternative Movement to deny science, rather than scientistic philosophy. Adam Smith, no less, was prescient in this respect. For him, the division of labour was not a good in itself, but the ingredient of an harmonious whole. That he saw the shadow falling is evident in this homely illustration from his *Moral Sentiments*:

> A watch that falls above two minutes in a day is despised by one curious in watches. He sells it perhaps for a couple of guineas, and purchases another at fifty, which will not lose above a minute in a fortnight. The sole use of watches, however, is to tell us what o'clock it is, and to hinder us from breaking any engagement, or suffering any other inconveniency by our ignorance in that particular point. But the person so nice with regard to this machine will not either be found more scrupulously punctual than other men, or anxiously concerned upon any other account to know precisely what time of day it is. What interests him is not so much the attainment of this piece of knowledge, as the perfection of the machine which serves to attain it

So, in our day, Schumacher has had to re-invent Appropriate Technology! Likewise, on a more sinister note, upon the testimony of none less than Lord Zuckerman (*The Times*, 19th January 1980), the nuclear establishment has taken over the atomic arms race, against the advice of the highest soldiers and statesmen in the land that more atomic power actually decreases national security. Because we know how to do it, it must be done. Those whom the gods destroy, they first make mad!

In the drive for knowledge, then, reductionism has taken charge. The technician is king, and specialization the norm. Consider the structure even of local government: it is neither local, nor government, because it has become just an amalgam of administratively convenient technical agencies. It is structured sectorally, according to the functions of education, health, transport, housing, etc. Political power runs along those various lines, and hardly crosses their committee boundaries—sometimes, as with police and water, lying outside the political structure altogether. In effect, there is no government of places, as such—and in consequence, there is less and less of place to govern. Yet, because place remains of abiding importance, offering identity, environmental groups focus on it, and this has led councillors to complain of their position being usurped. But this is bound to happen so long as councillors only represent the technologies of education, housing, etc. Local democracy, in fact, has become a euphemism.

The one activity of local government concerned with places as a whole is planning. Yet it too has succumbed to the requirements of its technique, to implementing regulations and to sustaining its professional status—in a field in which professionalism is an anachronism, since what is whole cannot be a specialist preserve. The language has not yet been fashioned by the Administration, in terms of which the whole can come before the parts: in which it can be claimed, say, that a village or town should determine what kind of school it should have, rather than let this be determined for it—or even have its school taken from it, thereby becoming the mere flotsam of this and other technologies. But then, technology in all its forms has torn our towns apart and spread them around, depriving all who live in them of their identities.

Identity, in fact, is crucial to this argument because it leads us to the counter-Enlightenment: the Romantic Movement. This Movement was spawned by the Age of Knowledge, in reaction against the impersonality of rationalism. For the knowledge that launched the Industrial Revolution also demonstrated what man could do to man: take away his very humanity, depersonalize and brutalize him, or at best treat people as if they were objects. The Romantic Movement thus re-invented the person: not the individual, as Locke and others of the Enlightenment had urged that concept, as a unit in the machine of society, but Natural Man, an autonomous being, not a creature of society but animated by his own spirit. (I say 're-invented'. for the conception of the person is at least as old as Christianity itself, or as perennial as the soul.) The Hero and the Artist were the quintessential people of romanticism and its forms; and in our own times the leader and the film star still fill this debased need. They stand outside the law so to speak, yet they too do not lack for certainty; indeed, the certainty of this personal kind of knowing locks them into the old paradigm. 'The heart has its reasons that reason knows not of,' and the artist is our licensed fool. Yet the world that this person of the Romantic Movement inhabited could not be a mechanistic one—for 'people' are not billiard balls— but was, rather, organic. Organicism was logically the concomitant of the romantic idea of the person, and out of it came the politics of nationalism, in Germany in particular.

Yet I would contend that the Enlightenment and the counter-Enlightenment, rationalism and romanticism, were parts of one syndrome, not separate paradigms. They were different sides of one coin, and they have combined to compose the climate of the times we have inherited. (The coin is that of the Self and the World: the same which Christianity struck in rendering to Caesar that which was Caesar's, and to God that which was God's: the religious, specifically the Christian, coin.) But they have not been good for one another, rationalism and romanticism; the coinage itself has become much debased. They tear our lives apart with schizophrenic force. The materialistic consumer society on the one hand, and the alienated arts—art feeding upon art—on the other: their separate certainties have conspired to leave us a wretched inheritance. They set each one of us apart from the world. Knowledge demands this detachment, because certainty cannot be had without it. You cannot be certain about the world if you are yourself part of it.

Marx has been so significant because his gigantic scenario was an attempt to resolve this classical dilemma within the framework of the paradigm of knowledge. It is interesting, in fact, that Marx both began and ended with the person—therein lay his romantic idealism—whilst, in between, he pronounced laws as implacable as any in the Old Testament. He began with an extended refutation of extreme solipsism, because he recognized the seduction of the very idea of the person that lay behind it, and from which his concept of alienation arose. In the end, however, Marx returned to that concern, with a kind of Rousseauesque Natural Man, free from institutional contamination—the State withered away—restored to himself again.

Significantly, the condition in between these two states of Utopia was one of process. Marx said that philosophers had explained the world, but the need was now to change it. This implied a different kind of knowledge: of knowing by doing, and in this also Marx was curiously prescient. For knowledge of process is arguably different from that kind of knowledge—the knowledge of things, of stuff—by which we have been lured. It implies, rather, an involvement with the thing that is changing, and is a step into the uncertain.

Marx's materialistic interpretation of history, however, provides only a half-way house out of the paradigm of knowledge. It sees history still as something apart, just as the empirical scientist sees the world apart, for Marx was still caught in the pattern of thought which strove for certainty. He made a material thing of process itself. Nevertheless, for all his old-fashioned idealism, he addressed himself to the question that remains central to our intelligence, at least since the rise of Christianity: the question of the Self and the World—the Person/Planet syndrome, in Theodore Roszak's terms. It is because it continues to do so, at least to some extent, that Marxism remains pertinent to a world fixated by the present paradigm.

The significance of the 'Green' movement in politics, indeed, lies precisely here. This movement began from concern for the environment. This was a direct challenge to reductionist thought because its concern is with the whole. Of course, the environmentalists' hostility was in the first instance directed against particular interests: the polluters. (Conversely, environmentalists have been accused with some justification of each merely defending his own green patch.) But at root we are all polluters, because that is how we have made sense of the world, by wasting it. We have learned to master the world—as the Enlightenment taught us we should— by considering it only part by part. Side-effects were not included in that calculus. Rather, separate power interests were built upon each such part, and our lives have been structured through an infinite regression of specialist occupations, no matter what violence is done to our very personalities thereby. Indeed, as for our identities, these could take care of themselves in our schizophrenic culture, so far as anyone not abandoned, as the hippies were, to an anti-social existence was concerned. In the face of all this, then, the environment—a totality, not a collection of parts—now forces itself upon our consciousness. We are being forced to recognize, that is, not only what man is doing to man under the thrall of knowledge, but what he is doing to Nature also.

Yet 'the environment' proves an elusive concept. It's as if it were everything, bar something. Given the challenge it makes to our accepted ways of making sense of the world, perhaps it is bound to be slippery. Yet how do we grasp this new kind of object?—for, as people speak of it, it is just another object. It exists regardless of those by whom it is created, for these have not caused it intentionally. It is a thing of itself. We still seek to understand it, that is to say, within the old paradigm: as something apart, perhaps even the sum of everything, about which there is simply knowledge to be had. This, at least, appears to be the view-point of ecology when it lays claim to being a new science. (Sometimes, sad to say, it seems to be a new king of determinism—full of the old certitude—yet one which presumes, not just a new paradigm of ideas, but a different kind of mind altogether. There is some danger, indeed, that if it is not to remain in the realms of mystification, ecology will become a new authoritarianism. Gregory Bateson and others have spoken of the need for us to think as Nature does. I sympathize, but I suspect there are still some steps to be taken before that happens. As Wittgenstein said: 'If lions could talk, we couldn't understand them'.) Perhaps, then, the environment is best considered, not for what it is, but in terms of how it might be understood.

The clue to this consists, prima facie, in the simple proposition that we have to learn again to live with Nature. The force of this proposition, after all, is hardly to be doubted. If we think we can remain the lords and masters of Nature, then the nuclear bind assuredly has us by the tail. The more we transform matter by this means, the more the risks of catastrophy multiply and the more extreme our precautions have to become. Those risks, in fact, extend beyond one generation to another. This is the peculiar horror of the environmental consequences of nuclear power, and it adds another dimension to 'the environment'; not even the dark Satanic mills of

the Industrial Revolution were such an affront to the innocence of babes unborn. However, to speak of living again with
Nature is to imply a radically different relationship to it. Our
present relationship is through detached measurement of it.
Indeed, have we not come to measure our very selves by
'growth'?—that is, by our success in using Nature, rather
than living with it?

Such a measure of ourselves was, of course, prog-
rammed in the Cartesian paradigm. If our approach to the
natural world is one of mastering it, and if we have fashioned
for ourselves the tools to accomplish this, our expectations of
such exploitation will logically be unlimited. Thus, indeed,
expectation has become our way of life; we have come to
measure the very validity of our lives by our success in
material growth. It would be fair to say, in fact, that ours has
become a politics of this 'growth': that political parties win or
lose by their promise or fulfilment of 'growth'—even though a
motor accident goes into GNP, and caring for one's family
does not. As this kind of 'growth', then, becomes not only
questionable, but unobtainable—as Nature takes her re-
venges—where will the parties find their rationale?

Shall a new romanticism—one of the environment—
come to hold the political stage? Could the parties make their
escape this way? Romanticism has indeed had significant
reinforcement of late. This has come, ironically, from science
itself, through research into the brain. We learn from this
research that the function of one hemisphere of the brain is
indeed with the forms of things, not their parts: with the
whole—the poem, not the words. The two hemispheres, in
fact, seem to match the two parts of the present paradigm of
knowledge—the Enlightenment and the counter-Enlightenment. Romanticism has thus received a legitimacy that
rationalism has sought to deny it. Intuition is hereby
endowed with as much credibility, as an instrument of the
truth, as is reasoned analysis. Indeed, the whole feminine ele-
ment in our lives is ratified from this source in a quite radical

way; the analytic intellect has thus superannuated itself. The contemporary disenchantment with rationalism, however, does not imply a rejection of the paradigm of knowledge itself and of its search for certainty. The environment (or the widespread concern for it) merely redresses the balance in the way that search is conducted.

Nevertheless, the momentum for a breakthrough to a way of living with, rather that mastering, Nature, and the method whereby the environment has to be understood, now plainly lies more with the intuitive and the personal: the rational is much discredited, along with all the social engineering which treats people as objects. This assertion is sympathetic to the kind of knowledge which comes from learning by doing. Indeed, this could be said to represent the romantic idea of knowledge itself, and it has close affinities with what used to be called 'progressive' education. This refers to schooling based upon the romantic idea of the child as a child—'child-centred' education—and its personal development: an idea stemming from Rousseau, who was of course the father of the Romantic Movement itself. Yet this focuses our difficulty into a microcosm: for no way has yet been found of marrying the two different educational regimes, the progressive and the conventional—that which is concerned with the child as a person, and that with it in society—in any one school. How, then, is the rising concern for the environment, with the immediacy of involvement in its processes that an understanding of it seems to demand, to be engaged with a political system that functions on rational lines?

One way of not achieving this, to be sure, is by establishing a Department of the Environment: the solution by institution. So long as the language spoken in that Department remains—as it does—the language of finance and administration, nothing but harm can be done by such an organization. The post-war generation of Whitehall administrators has—not perhaps wilfully, but from lack of comprehension—set about destroying the holistic seed of planning, of seeing a place as a place, that was begining to grow in their midst. Ironically, it was not until James Callaghan as Prime Minister began dismantling the D o E by taking the Ministry of Transport out of it again, that Government pronouncements on transport began to take on an environmental tone. Presumably that Ministry then no longer felt it had to defend its technical corner. In fact, an effective concern for the environment at government level must presume some rightness between the forms of our everyday affairs and the technologies that serve them. But what a world this speaks of! In it, all technology would be appropriate technology: the feminine principle would have as much impact upon public life as the masculine: quality would hold sway against quantity: art and science would no more be estranged. This is to imagine a world in which our lives would be quite re-ordered. It is inconceivable, however, that this could happen within the present paradigm.

Yet environmentalism, as I've sought to argue, on the whole is of the present paradigm. It may be an approach to the new politics, therefore, but it is not that politics itself. Nor is there conceivably room for a whole new dimension of romanticism, such as environmentalism is, within our present politics, fixed as this so firmly is in the rationalistic mould. The fiascos of cost-benefit analysis have demonstrated the limits of the system. To think otherwise may indeed prove the downfall of those who would form new 'Green' parties within the present system. In this difficulty, then, we could do worse than turn to Fritz Schumacher for guidance. For Schumacher, if anyone, was the prophet of the Alternative Movement, and he disavowed mere environmentalism. His themes, rather, were appropriate technology—technology that fitted a way of life, rather than the converse—the human ('small') scale in all possible organizations, and what he called 'good work'—that is, ultimately, a relationship between a person and the world that was right for them both. At the centre of it all he put a spiritual concern: the question of what animates us, for without this nothing is real. In so doing, he was explicit that the Cartesian paradigm, with its devitalised dimension of things and their quantities, lacking the qualitative dimension to bring it back to life, was played out. He saw that we have put a torch into a blind man's hand, and called it the Enlightenment. Schumacher's concerns, in fact, were not with knowledge, but with what knowledge means. He dared to conceive that there might be meaningless knowledge. He proclaimed, in brief, the shift of paradigm: from knowledge, to meaning.

Descartes opened the Age of Knowledge by positing his method on the certainty that God would not deceive us about the mathematical rules that Creation obeyed. Perhaps Einstein closed that Age with his despairing comment on Quantum Theory, to which (we are told) he was never reconciled: 'God does not play dice with the Universe'. The signs multiply, in fact, that Certainty itself has been deposed. And if Certainty has been deposed, knowledge is not Knowledge any more. Or, at least, knowledge must change its significance. There is more at issue, it seems, in our relationship with the world, than that search for certainty by which we have so far been driven.

Yet how fixed in certainty our politics has become! To establish it, not only have whole political parties grown, but ideologies are embedded in them. These ideologies are abstract systems, sets of logically consistent ideals, with the objective authority of law, governing all our conduct, pronouncing apparent truth about society: about how society must operate if such truth is to endure. As systems, they furnish certainty in the way the behaviour of the parts is interpreted. Their internal logic (and this alone) gives them their strength in a world crumbling under its own structural failure; and the models they take for human nature, being idealizations, are unexaminable. They are more lethal than any physical danger the world holds, because their logic would enslave us. Yet they have our political system increasingly in their grip. They are the last debt we must pay to the paradigm of Knowledge.

## The Politics of Meaning

It has to be brought home, the immensity of this shift. Otherwise, we shall be at the mercy of events—and the more cruel their lessons will be. Our culture has not, of course, been without its blessings; to have lived off the capital of the earth and not benefited from it, after all, would have been shame indeed. Freedom from bigotry has been one of these blessings, for all our pursuit of certainty. Will our climate remain sufficiently pragmatic, then, for the commonsense of the great majority to keep the zealots at bay? To exercise commonsense, enough of us need to be able to read the sign-posts that will get us from place to place, giving us our bearings in ordinary life. But when the signs are in a new language—when they no longer speak of jobs, or growth, or lawfulness—it will be easy to lose direction.

This direction could readily be recovered, perhaps, were the shift of paradigm a minor one: but it is not. The Age of Knowledge itself was a shift from the Renaissance (for which the classical world had provided a passing model for man's minds) and so on regressively, to the origins of Western civilisation. But all of that was within the context of dualistic thought—whether Plato's, or Christianity's, or Descartes'—for this is the very characteristic of the West. Such thinking is endemic in us. What is so extraordinary about our present condition, then, is that, facing a world increasingly used up, we have come to the end of the road of dualism. To be its lord and master is to be sovereign only over its depletion. This being so, the shift of paradigm is immense. Perhaps it can only be measured by the nuclear holocaust implicit in the present dispensation. That is the order of magnitude of the desert to which dualism has brought us.

Is this hyperbole—or are not many of us now resigned to the probability, amounting to inevitability, of atomic warfare if nothing really changes? Such an event would be in the logic, no less, of the dualistic assumptions we make about the world. We can hardly allow, surely, that such a cataclysm might ensue merely from our everyday practices themselves; they are not in themselves all that foolish. Yet that logic leads inexorably back to idealism. Idealistic thought is like the spectacles we see the world through, and never take off the ends of our noses. It is the archetypal dualism of the Western mind: namely, concerning those forms of which we have 'true' knowledge, in contrast to the stuff of which we have only transient sensations. Utopias are conceived from this principle, and our best spirits have been dedicated to it. Yet the evidence is now cumulative, that it is not false ideals that have brought us to our present pass, but idealism itself: the very certainty it presumes, and the detachment of the idealist from the actual world. This, however, is the hardest thing to persuade people of : one's seriousness in saying that idealism is dead.

Perhaps this difficulty illustrates the immensity of the shift that is upon us. What will ever convince people of it? Perhaps resurgent Islam will by now have sufficiently roused their curiosity. If we try to interpret this phenomenon in our own language, however, we do so at our peril. If we think of it simply as revenge for past humiliations, say, or as an irrational response to Western technological pre-eminence, we shall deserve to stew in our own juice. Islam, in its own language, is simply a rejection of the division of God: of the Trinity, therefore, which, with the Church mediating between Father and Son, was the elegant Christian solution to the perennial human problem of the self and the World. Yet the Trinity was the great heresy against (in the marvellous Koranic phrase) the Peoples of the Book.

We can respect the incredible effrontery of the Christian

solution—this reconciliation of Jewery and of the Greeks, of Babylon and Egypt: of having our cake, and eating it—all the more now that its authority is vanishing. This dualism, however, set man off against the world, encouraging his mastery of it. The Christian's stance is one of stewardship of the earth, yet nevertheless apart from it. Any suggestion of animism—that all created things are part of God's Holy Mountain—is heresy. Man has a special place in the Christian universe, and when Isiah says 'and a little child shall lead them', this is taken to refer to the infant Jesus, rather than to truth innocently perceived. It is well understood that Christianity has had difficulty in accommodating to environmentalism just as it had in assimilating St. Francis. If the Christian God is indeed not dead, this above all is the challenge which that faith must meet. Only the Church can do so—for faith itself rests upon authority—but, precisely, which church?

Yet it is this distance between man and the world that has given the West its mastery over Nature. The monasteries were the forerunners of the West's technology. And it is this very distance that Islam rejects. The means by which it does so is activism: the pursuit of that kind of knowledge which comes from being part of, rather than apart from, the world. (Shades of Marx!—but, after all, Islam is a way of life, not a religion.) By contrast, the Christian exploration of the world is antipathetic to Islam. If Islam is resurgent south of the Sahara and elsewhere, for instance, it may be that Christianity is seen there to carry the germ of the world's destruction with it because God has been divided. We should at least be wise to note the deep chord this strikes amongst some peoples today.

This is not to say we should embrace (though we should understand) Islam. Much more fundamentally, the same standpoint is evident in our indigenous thought. It is now almost commonplace, for instance, that the distinction between observer and observed no longer holds true: that observation affects what is observed. The same ferment is at work in philosophy. This, in fact, is the signpost of the great divide between our paradigms. And it is comparable in its depth at least to the divide between Aristotelian and Newtonian physics—the difference between the appearance of objects at rest and an equilibrium of forces bearing upon them. For philosophy today is insisting that language does not reflect reality (as hitherto taken for granted) but itself modifies what we apprehend, and is not just the currency in which we must transact.

Humans with the command of words have assumed these give us access to reality. Such is the power of the Name! It generates 'things', and all their grammar: hence also the notion of reality itself, and physics and materiality—and certainty! But it is not so. We are in as incomprehensible a mystery as ever, and the mystics are our only true realists. They alone use words to see through words. Otherwise, so far as 'reality' is concerned, we remain at one with the brutes. We differ from them, perhaps, only in our appreciation itself of the mystery. Man is thus not just 'homo ludens', rather than 'homo sapiens', but the player of language games. The philosophical puzzle has been the relationship between words, as the vehicles of our thoughts, and the profoundly mysterious universe we so carelessly inhabit. Simultaneously, the ultimate reality science so assiduously pursues into the stuff of matter is turning out, in the realm of sub-particle physics, to be not matter at all, but process. What all this at last brings into question, then, is idealism itself.

Yet most politicians today probably like to think of themselves as idealists. Idealism is arguably the primary urge of politics and our society is still indulgent towards the idealist, no matter how confused he may be. It would be thought improper to suggest in most circles that idealistic thinking is just a pseudonym for itellectual muddle. We have so long been indulgent of Plato's tyrant, the philosopher-king, that when, in our own century, those ultimate products of the idealistic mind, Stalin and Hitler, bestrode the world, we repressed the truth about our complicity in them. Such has been the power of pure knowledge over our minds!

Perhaps this is not surprising, since the main repository of pure knowledge is our universities, with their eremitic traditions. Pure knowledge, however, seems to be a peculiarly English value, and perhaps this has something to do with the long dissociation in England between knowledge and work. (We are governed, not so much by mandarins, as Brahmins.) Be that as it may, political idealism would be relatively harmless were that where matters rested. But it is in the Civil Service that our active philosopher-kings are to be found today.

Bureaucracy—the suffocating blanket of today's bureaucracy, at least—is the main creditor of idealism. Bureaucracy is the agent of political idealism; we conceive of the impossible, and we ask bureaucracy to achieve it. Bureaucracy becomes malignant—having a parasitical life of its own—when the aspirations of politicians became hopelessly idealistic. Those familiarly cloudy policies, with their turgid legislation, in fact, would matter less were there not a corps of beings at hand, full of self-confidence that it can translate the impractical into the practical: that a good Platonist, in other words, can administer an ideal world. Nothing but idealism, surely—the deepest foundation of our culture— could sustain so many decent people in such untenable situations of their own contriving: untenable in terms of ordinary and compassionate relationships, person to person. Our bureaucrats must despairingly console themselves that they are bringing a better world about.

It may be said that idealism is not to be construed as expounded here but, rather, retains its everyday validity simply as an aspiration for the ultimate. But I am not arguing, say, that the best is the enemy of the good. To aspire is not to idealize (nor is aspiration quite what one associates with bureaucracy, as an agent of idealism). The contention is, simply, that we idealize our aspirations, and that we do so because we are in thrall to this delusion: and that, in being driven by certainty to do this, not only have our liabilities in human terms now exceeded our assets to the point of bankruptcy, but (the ultimate irony) confusion is the only outcome. If, then, certainty is the source of so confused a world, could uncertainty be worse?

It seems curious in the perspective of Copernicus—of the earth as a speck in the abyss—that certainty should so long have ruled our minds. Anyway, the reign of certainty is now coming to an end, and perhaps, all things considered, the time-lag has not been so very protracted; it has been said that scientists today still act out their own lives as if Newton had said the last word. Uncertainty, then, is what underlies the notion of the language-game, which entwines in one thread the constant interplay between the world and our thoughts about it. This central notion of twentieth century philosophy implies neither finality, nor causality. It bespeaks process, and involvement therein, rather than knowledge about the stuff of the world. Meaning, rather, takes the centre of its stage: not meaning in some semantic sense, however, but of what part language is playing at any moment in our lives. Meaning, in this sense, can never be fixed, but will always depend upon circumstances.

So if politics is to be attuned to the changing climate of thought, it too must arguably be about meaning. That is to say, for instance, it must be about a scale of things that makes common sense to people: an everyday sense, that is, not of the grandiose: a sense, rather, of what is appropriate. This is as much as to say, then: throw away your ideologies! We shall not need such crutches any more. Politicians will have to ask questions, not about which ideal society does such and such a measure serve, but what will it mean for the quality of the lives of those it affects?

The meaning lies in the use. Does 'welfare' mean a compassionate society, or in reality some confrontation with a soulless official in his bleak surroundings? This suggests, say, that politics should start from where people live: from places, as places. It should likewise be about the work people do, as work: as what that work means to people, therefore, not as an alienated activity for which only the wage supplies the rationale: for the meaning it has, therefore, as a transaction between the worker and the world—and not just for the doer of it either, but for the users of the artifact or service concerned, as meaningful to them. These may seem like the simplistic questions children, rather than sophisticated analysts, frame about life. but perhaps they are also the questions which that child in Isiah would have asked. And they are certainly the sort of questions young people today are finding the courage to ask. Such people have experienced the plastic society, and the senselessness of what is expected of them in it. They are going back to the beginning, to find the meanings.

Language (the sharing of which is our true democracy) gives us the forms of everyday life. Meanings are to do with the forms, or patterns, of events. There are whole areas of discourse, however, each with its grammar, for whose forms no further explanations are to be had. Such are the forms of life itself, each one a language, and to be accepted as they are. They constitute separate areas of judgement, each with its own currency of speech, and one of the crasser fallacies of idealism (and ideology) has been to assume these can somehow all be reduced to a common denominator: to money, for instance, which supposedly can measure the values of art, or the quality of urban life, or the worth of a person. If politics is to be about meaning, then, it must be structured in terms of these various forms which confer meaning upon our everyday lives.

What are these forms? The currency perhaps, provides one. The language of the law is another: all the forms of justice. And so on, including diplomacy, defence, etc. However, the form of life that perhaps carries most meaning for people but to which, because it has been made subordinate to all manner of technologies, politics pays least attention, is that of our everyday surroundings: the places where we live. (At least, small attention is paid to this in the media at the national, or centralized, level; but in the local press of course it receives the most notice.) Most emphatically, this is not to recommend a stronger Department of Local Government. Conversely, however, and by the same token, the repercussions upon all other areas of politics of giving local life the attention it calls for would be considerable and imponderable: upon fiscal policies, for instance, and all kinds of centrally imposed technical standards. What it implies, certainly, is a Britain of local identities.

Such a suggestion might have seemed insane not long ago. The Englishman, except in war-time, had almost forgotten what his nationality meant. He governed an Empire and did it quite anonymously, being himself of a racial melting-pot, and did not feel himself to be as other men are. The world was his parish. But now that our horizons have shrunk, not only the Welsh and the Scots, but the Englishman also is feeling in his bones the need for more local identity. His misfortune is, that he cannot so easily find it in the England across which the accent of the upper classes has cast its bland spell. Yet even for him, his regional roots are still there to be found.

This, however, is to look at matters from the centre out, as a question of decentralization. It is as much from the person, rather, that meaning stems. (It is he or she, after all, who speaks the language in which meanings are expressed, and whose life is bound into that process.) Any politics of meaning, therefore, must concern the forms of everyday life and stand the test of being appropriate to these. This implies a politics of community, of the patterns that hold people together. This stands in contrast to the politics of today—the politics of the Consumer Society—which is focussed upon the particulate and quantitative: upon the provision of one new technical innovation or another, like those decadent Athenians of long ago who were forever seeking after some new thing, We, like them, have lost the polis, and it will be the prime task of a new politics to recover it.

Or it may be truer, that politics has rejected us. Perhaps, at root, we lost the polis because we mixed it with Utopia. It was not enough for us to render unto Caesar that which is Caesar's; the coin had to be two-sided. Machiavelli has still not been forgiven in the moralistic English-speaking world, with its lack of political realism, for pointing out the miseries to which this mixing of values must lead: the hypocrisies, unction and perfidy. (If one deceives oneself that one's service to God is a service to Mammon, however, this tends to be the result.) In consequence, perhaps, the notion that there might be real communities again seems impossibly remote to us. We have an education system, after all, which assumes that knowledge is contained in 'subjects' and which, following the logic of that premise, unconcernedly sacrifices communities to the rationalization of its schools. (The same thinking is true of all departments of government, each in its way.) The paraphernalia of Utopia consorts ill with the real life of a community. There is a small place for actual people in the politics of Utopia.

How, then, shall we re-discover the polis? This is as much as to ask, how shall we make politics an honourable business again? How shall it be about the meanings life holds, instead of a game of shadows, played cynically for power itself? An alternative Utopia is assuredly not the answer. That would compound our errors: there is no 'Green Utopia' on offer. Nor would political revolution serve, for that is part of the naturalistic fallacy—like the fallacy of egalitarianism that, as moral beings, all men are also materially equal: for the revolution in process is much more than political. A Green politics, rather, would start with politicians asking them-selves a different sort of questions: questions, simply, about what things mean, rather than whether they bespeak some sort of truth. The politicians who asked this kind of question would be a different breed from those we now condone, the ideologists. They would not be great theorists, but perhaps more like, say Wilberforce. He was not the originator of any system of political ideas, or the leader of his country; he only freed the slaves. Nor is this to say we should all retire to our parishes. It was said of Medieval man that he lived in a village, but partook of Christendom. Even more so today, spiritually the world belongs to us all.

A politics of meaning is one which focusses upon forms of life with which we can be comfortable: upon communities, therefore, that are actual. This is to speak of a social metamorphosis, but one in which it is possible to believe. This possibility, however, is contained in the unspoken premise of all that has gone before, of the reality of the spiritual. Whereas this premise is absent from the politics of Knowledge (being replaced by Utopianism) to a politics of Meaning it is integral. If where one is and what one does is to have meaning, the forms life takes cannot be profane.

# OF TOWNS, TONGUES AND TAXES

There are much deeper questions at issue than have yet been aired in the public debate over the Government's attempt to limit the powers of local authorities in Britain. Even the unease, indeed revolt, of some of the Government's most eminent supporters has not brought these questions to the surface. Nor is this really surprising, for what is ultimately at issue is the compatibility of the Nation State—to which all our politicians adhere—with the forms of life of a post-industrial society. The Government's measures are a long step towards a pervasive control over our lives, by which alone the Nation State might be enabled to survive.

The issue is clouded by the fact—of which nobody likes to make mention—that local government does not exist. What exists, actually, are a set of agencies for the administration of statutory functions: bodies of convenience. 'Local Government' was invented in Britain barely a hundred years ago (by the Local Government Act of 1888). True, it was largely, and romantically based on a folk memory of the ancient shires. There was no question, at the time, however, of some popular revival of these bodies to counter the spreading power of the centre. Rather, those ancient earldoms were resurrected to serve the centre once again—and suitably given some modern shreds of democracy to wear. The invention of Local Government was thus never conceived as a threat to Britain's 'unitary State' (as the upholders of the centre like to call our present constitutional arrangements): on the contrary, it was conceived as an actual instrument of the State.

And yet, an unspoken compact had existed for two hundred years—really, ever since the Bill of Rights—between the centre and the forces of local life. Those forces, in Britain, were of course primarily represented by the gentry, in the form particularly of Justices of the Peace. The Bill of Rights itself—the nearest Britain comes to a Constitution—was a charter of individualism within the given fact of the Nation State. And for many decades the gentry still effectively controlled Local Government itself. The growth of industrial cities, of course, is what upset this cosy arrangement, primarily because of the need to get children off the streets and into what is called 'education'—by contrast, that is, with the school of life that had served them hitherto.

This kind of State was itself a concomitant of the Enlightenment: its power was thus founded on knowledge, and that 'knowledge', being of the sort that is external to the observer, puts a premium on the descriptive powers of any use of language—nay, on language itself. The common tongue, from being a medium of culture, became an instrument of power.

The language of government itself inevitably became increasingly arcane, taking upon itself the lost authority of Latin. 'It seems', said Sir Thomas More, in the middle of the seventeenth century, 'that we must all learn Latin'—meaning, that the new-found energy of Renaissance English was already succumbing to the technical exactitudes of the new knowledge, its resonances constrained by the new dictionaries. This process of holding power has gone on, down to this day, whether in the mystical gobbledegook of economic policy, or in the jargon of beaurocracy at large.

Yet, if 'knowledge' were no longer power—what then? Indeed, if observer and observed are no longer separable, and language therefore not the instrument of truth, what becomes of the State as we know it, whose authority rests upon the mystique of a common language? What becomes of all those 'standards' by which the State would bond us together—of all the realms in which technology is king? In the new paradigm, now upon us, those politically suppressed forces of local life—how, through what structures, shall they assert themselves? and how is our tongue to be restored to its cultural, from its political, primacy? How is it to be reclaimed by people in their ordinary lives? How, in other words is the inexorable centralization which 'knowledge' has imposed, to be reversed?

The fact is, there is little enough to be done. It must largely happen of itself, this breakdown of the Nation State. The flawed social engineering of monetarism, with its facile notion of what people are—of Economic Man—points to the alienation at the roots of inflation: to the distance of responsibility people feel, not just from the currency itself, but from the currency of speech about it—with its P S B R, its G N P, its M1, M2, M3 and now (praise be!) M zero, meaning nothing. No wonder the contradictions of our society grow!—not just the contradiction between work and the workless, or between Governments wanting to spend less whilst inexorably spending more, but between an expressed wish to leave people to manage their own affairs whilst acutally controlling them more and more from the centre. For money rules all public policy, not because of the virtues of economy, but because it is quantitative: it deals in the measurable, and therefore in the external truths, the 'knowledge',upon which the Nation State is founded. So, like an aircraft in a tail-spin, the more we seek to control this Nation State the more assured its break-up becomes.

In these circumstances, then, the most we can do is to prepare the ground for the Local State to follow, as follow it must. The reform of local government is no longer of serious concern, but rather that of the State itself. We have, however, no tradition of commune, or Gemeinde, in Britain; the medieval commons were long since absorbed into the Commons itself. Nor do we entrust our local authorities, such as they are, even with the functions normal to local life elsewhere in the world— police, health, water and sewerage; and the rationale of our system rests in nothing but the mere provision of services, not with identity at all. So we have to start from the beginning—and the best way to do this is with our eyes open.

Of course, a certain start has already been made. We have invented 'the environment'. We had to do this to provide a context that would restore some meaning to our lives: one that would give us back a lost identity. (This is why the 'environmentalists' are not beloved of local authorities, whose pitch they queer.) Beyond this, however, we should above all take a look at our cities, to see what they really are.

It is perhaps asking a great deal to accept that our cities have become meaningless, whether as places or communities (except as nihilistic communities of despair). Yet what are they but mere residues of how we live? The State, moreover, has taken politics from local life, and the State is seizing up. So it can be no easy matter, given the technological complexity of these times, to rediscover a credible politics of local life, and of our formless cities in particular.

Perhaps, then, the process has to start from a recognition that cities have become instruments of oppression. They trap humans, as a snare traps any creature led on by its appetite. If we have difficulty in seeing this it is surely because we also share those appetites, taking them for granted. They stem from our unquestioned assumption, that the world is there for us to exploit: in a word, from our dualism, our apartness from the world. Cities, then, are where the 'wealth' that the world supposedly yields up to our intelligence is to be made.

Alas! for the mockery cities have made of that very concept. Millions are paying for 'wealth', streets paved with gold, through the degradation of their lives, through the loss of their dignities. And, in Britain's case, policies of shoring up the inner cities amount to a conspiracy for the perpetuation of that servitude to the myth of wealth: a 'conspiracy' because it suits the politics of our centralized state to keep the cities as prisons for the poor. It suits both those who want to manipulate the poor for reasons of power, and those who want to keep them from the preserves of the rich.

We live in the midst of a tragedy we had thought was to be our inheritance. It should chasten us to realize that there may be problems for which there are no solutions: that techniques and mechanics may not work. Of course, it is admirable to succour those who fall by the wayside of our march to riches. But when they ungratefully vandalise the provision we have made for them in which to live out their lives—the kept places of the poor, which is the use we have found for our cities—are we not obliged to question our 'charity': nay, that march itself?

It is true that the poor who do escape from our cities—as a few have done through the New Towns programme—are none the less in pursuit of materialism. We are not, at any stroke of social mechanics, going to eliminate the desire for possession of things, engrained in our very assumptions about life. In time, no doubt, we shall have to learn again to live with the world (and one another): not crudely to dominate it—barbarizing ourselves in the process—by our detachment from it. That lesson, however, will remain forever unlearnable, barring some holocaust, in the hostile environment of our cities. It might therefore, at the very least, be a step in the direction of community, and hence of the Local State, if the cities' roots of oppression were destroyed.

These roots must be traced to the values of city land. It is these values which lead to the competition for space in which the poor are inescapably the losers: 'inescapably', not just because they are crammed into miserable accommodation and made victims of the dreadful politics of urban housing, but because the costs of escaping are driven ever higher. Those who can afford to do so, leave: and are leaving our Londons, Liverpools, Manchesters, etc., in their hundreds of thousands annually and of their own accord. But those, who, by the rising costs and impediments of this exodus itself, cannot leave, become ever more impoverished by the pressures of the centre: of the fashionable world of urban life, with its restless knowledge of each new thing and the illusory excitement of pursuing it. They become, in fact, the detritus of our ruling fallacy of knowledge itself, of what it supposedly is to 'know' something. Cities are but the meretricious product of that self-illusion of Man as the Lord and Master of Nature. They have become manifestations of the penalty for that humanistic hubris.

It is really no coincidence that derelict cities and centralized power are twin symptoms of the sickness of these times. They are each in their way monuments to the disease of greed, of possession over things, and the power this encourages. It is a disease to which Britain has been peculiarly prone, both because of the very descriptive power of the English language, and because—perhaps since the Norman Conquest—the resistant instinctual force of local political life is historically lacking. Whilst, then, it could be fascinating, if abstruse, to speculate about what might become of our language, there are practical possibilities of action at least to be held in store till the time comes for the regeneration of local life.

Cities have become instruments of oppression because the values generated by their very development have not inhered in their communities, but have disappeared into remote pockets. They have never become communities as a result, but just fragmented conglomerations. Had those values stayed with the people who generated them, they would have been used to provide their own services: their own schools, their own hospitals, their own parks—instead of, at best, the crumbs that have fallen from local rich men's tables, or the tables of kings, or of what governments or local commissars have imposed. Community is locked in the land, and the key has long since been lost.

This, of course, is why the right to levy rates is of such emotional importance. It is the vestigial symbol of local identity, just as it is the only way in which any local authority can even touch the value of its land. Admittedly, there is, by now, everything possible wrong with the mechanics of taxation by rates; further to restrict their use, however, would be a retrograde step. If we want people to be responsible about money—and if inflation is a function of that kind of irresponsibility—the wealth that lies closest to people must be at their discretion. After several centuries of neglect of this elementary truth, then, there is in principle only one way of rectifying the now dangerous consequences of the State's growing usurpation of authority over our lives. The State—the chastened State I envisage—should be obliged to endow from its general revenues local authorities (even the local authorities we've got) with sums equivalent to the annualized property values of their areas. In other words, the rents, as well as the rates. After all, this is just what happens (albeit uniquely) at Letchworth, the first Garden City.

The logic of this step would, naturally, and in short order, lead to radical changes of structure. There would, for instance, be a reconsideration of the kind of local authorities we now have—authorities which are at present merely catchment areas for the delivery of statutory services, not communities at all. There would be a fundamental dismantling of Whitehall—leaving it, perhaps, only with national defence and foreign policy. And there would be a total re-appraisal of taxation itself, etc.

All this, admittedly, is day-dreaming. The Nation State must first dismember itself. However, if one were asked what if anything could be done now to bring about desirable change, one would point in a most unlikely direction. This is suggested by the root change in values between the Nation and the Local State. From the rational idealism (and its conjoint materialism) of the former there must be a change—but to what? I think it can be only to an aesthetic of life: from the good (and equally from Original Sin) to whatsoever is seemly. You may say, we have left all that behind! Of course: and where? In classical Greece: that is, in the very roots of our civilization. The same values, however, happen still to be the ruling force in Japan: and Japan . . . well, even in our own materialistic terms, it seems to have something to say to us— not least, as a matter of fact, because of the allusive, rather than the descriptive power of its language. (To the Japanese, the very descriptive power of English is mere crudity.) Where else indeed have we to go, discredited as our culture is, but away from idealism and towards what, instinctively, is seemly: away, above all, from the brutal ugliness of our cities?

The 'arts' as we have them in their esoteric forms, of course, share in that discredit. They are but a function of our materialism: the other side of that coin. But it is still through art that identity can be reached—and perhaps gardening, say, or cooking, will prove to be the true art of the future. Certainly, the thirst for identity is the time-bomb underneath the Nation State. That, indeed, is why there are signs of hope in the way the people of Glasgow are taking their city back from its commissars. Another bloodless British revolution on the way?

Now, if anyone (apart from the mandarins themselves) doubts the competence of people to run their own lives in the way all this implies, perhaps they should be reminded that in the not uncivilized country of Switzerland the communes, with an average population of less that 1,500 souls, raise and dispose of one third of the country's public expenditure, and the cantons—far smaller, on average, than our counties—of another third: leaving the State itself, and only by discretion of the cantons, with the rest. Whether the mandarins believe it or not, the Swiss even dispense with a Ministry of

Education—amongst others! But then, Switzerland has no ruling language: just as, conversely, if incidentally, India to its disgrace makes English its ruling language, and so misrules its plethora of peoples.

Of course, if all these changes came about we should not in due course have the cities we know—and which are the shame of Europe: nor the governments. But we should be able to hold up our heads again.

# RETROSPECT AND PROSPECT

We hear on every side—even, at last, in Britain—that all the parties are seeking the Green vote. One may be forgiven for being the more on one's guard. The superficiality of it all— the mouthing by party leaders of slogans ('We do not inherit the earth: we borrow it from our children', etc.) that once had the ring of truth when spoken by those who minted them ten or twenty years ago—this is not so much what is distressing, as the threat to the spirit of the Green movement. For, paradoxically, the Green movement itself has lost, if not its way, certainly its momentum. The conditions for a hijack exist.

Were this just a question of the force of that movement passing into the mainstream of society, one would not have cause for complaint. Certainly, purism about 'greeness' should not enter into the question. Yet one rememebers how, once, Christianity was suborned by Rome—how it was used by Constantine and his successors: and one is troubled.

Christianity, which marked a huge shift in comprehension by an equally ravaged world, was hopelessly (and murderously) divided between the Athanasians and the Arians—between belief in the Trinity as the model of reality, and the indivisibility of God: between the authority of the Church, and of inner truth—so that in its division it became the pawn of a rotten Empire. It did not save or change that

Empire, but condoned its dying spasms. The analogy between that piece of history and our situation today is not so
far-fetched. It is less the drained strength of a threatened
civilization than the indecisiveness of the alternative to it that
accounts for one's pessimism about how things now stand.

Now, when I speak of the 'Green movement' I am talking
of the political and social dimension of the new paradigm of
thought. Its prophet was, above all, Schumacher—though
there were others as important as he in forging the mould.
This pardigm itself, of course, is profoundly influenced by the
new physics of Quantum Mechanics—with a bow towards
the 'non-observing self' long known to Buddhist thought—as
also by the later philisophy (after his recantation) of
Wittgenstein, as well as by ecology, and so forth; and the
Green movement stands to it all in much the same analogous
relationship as Hobbes (and hence the Nation State) once
stood to Galileo and his Laws of Motion. Yet the division in
the Green movement is as persistent as that which has flawed
each succeeding shift of pattern, from the time of Christianity
itself onwards.

I am referring, in the first instance, to the strain of
millenarianism strongly evident in the Green movement.
This idea of a New Age, of a Second Coming, is, alas! perhaps
endemic in the West. Our tradition, it almost seems, cannot
do without divine intervention, if only harmony by the will of
God is to be attained in life on earth. This notion, after all, is
virtually inherent in that of God itself: certainly of quasi-
divinized Mankind. It could be said to be the motive force of
Christian culture and hence, however illusory it might be,
claimed that we have no option but to embrace it. To do
otherwise, after all, would be to wipe the slate clean, to deny
our culture and its true riches: but that, surely, we could not
do. And yet, this question will not leave us in peace; and, if
merely to vary the pattern were only to compound the
problem—if, even with a respite of a hundred years, it were to
make our last condition still worse than our first, and the dis-

harmony of (Western) Mankind in the midst of Creation yet greater—then perhaps some other force than millenarianism must be harnessed.

To put it differently, perhaps Toynbee was right in saying that the most important event of the Twentieth Century has been the coming of Buddhism to the West. I do not note this to proselytize (I would not know how to do so; though I would take issue with those Western liberals who ironically seem to have put on the missionaries' mantle in decrying any other culture than their own), but I say it only to suggest the scale of the problem. Nor would I be diverted by any talk of the essential unity of all faiths: for by their fruits they shall be known. I only want to avow that, scratch many a 'green', and you'll find a millenarian underneath: and that, not only is this off-putting to a basically sympathetic public, but—as the record of European Green politics all too clearly shows— distasteful to many another 'green', not least those with a different notion of a Green heaven. It also, to be personal, makes the Green movement a somewhat prickly lot to handle!

To this main strain of apocalyptic Green thought, of course, other facets could be added. There is, for instance, the school of Armageddon, which, though it has enormously raised our consciousness of nuclear war, makes any calm discussion about international affairs impossible; and then there are those implicitly hostile to new technologies—although to them much credit is due for having counterbalanced a once universal belief in the technological fix. (If we hear less of this fix nowadays from high political circles, it may be the best of evidence that a Green consciousness is spreading.) However, the other side of the division in the Green movement is represented by nothing but the fragments of which it is compounded. The seperateness of these activities each from the other—though all attest to some important common ground, some change of climate—is as much a structural weakness as is millenarianism.

The weakness of this one-eyed, one-off approach to Green issues—be it, say, the protection of wild-life, or advocacy of open government, or opposition to Cruise missiles—is not just that it leaves untouched the heart of the matter, the roots of our present condition: but rather that, being itself precisely unecological, it even aggravates our general condition. Protectors of the countryside, for instance, care little for the cities, and understand them and their inhabitants less: whilst protagonists of open government leave unasked the abiding question of the centralizing and therefore secretive, forces in our society.

Categorically, this is not to imply that to all social questions there is one, and only one, Green solution. The balance between wild-life and human aspirations, for instance, will no doubt always be disputable. What matters is the balance itself, rather than Descartes' assertion that Man should become 'The Lord and Master of Nature'. The corruption, however, within the bud of any one-eyed Green campaign is, as it was in Classical times, with those 'forever seeking after some new thing': namely, in its vunerability to appropriation by the sensationalizing 'media.' For the shallow perspective which that very word bespeaks carries no intimation of change: no change of pattern, that is, for such change must come at many related points, simultaneously, and out of the depths. It was, after all, the strength of Schumacher that he could see the whole—the technological, the social, the philosophical: all of a piece. Those Greens who cannot see the whole are flawed.

Between millenarianism, then, and at best a sort of Green opportunism, what course is open? This question might helpfully be put another way. In our times, we have virtually invented 'the environment'. However, does this signify a paradise lost? or is it merely something necessary in order to give some meaning to our lives? I would opt for the latter: and I would do so because, for me, it has been the replacement, at the centre of our lives, of meaning by knowledge that accounts for our present untenable predicament. ('Alienation' is perhaps a more fashionable—yet insufficient—mode of discourse for all this.) The point is that by our knowledge we have but fragmented the world and, the trust we put in Providence having long since faded, the task is to achieve coherence again. This predicates neither the making of Utopia, nor mere *ad hoc* practicality. It signifies, rather, the evolution of another way of life, one which would be implicate in our ordinary practices.

The politics of knowledge, let us be clear, is concerned with the distribution of the fruits of technology—all within a context which assures that the power of that distribution rests within the State. In so doing, for instance, the State determines what passes for 'education,' for it is as fodder for the machine that this kind of politics treats young people. And if the politics of knowledge generates (as it does) both irreperable and insoluble dislocations of social structure—like unemployment/inflation—and concomitant irresponsibility about the surroundings upon which we are personally dependent, well, this is only to be expected of a dualistic culture like ours, in which the very notion of knowledge derives from the divisibility of matter. In what, then, might a converse politics of meaning consist?

Meaning lies in pattern. A politics of meaning, therefore, must lie in the search for patterns of life that bestow meaning. This speaks of the importance of connections: it says that it must be evident to all involved with such a politics how any one thing connects with another. Thus, for example, in such politics education would not be an abstraction imposed from outside, determined by 'subjects' into which life is most dubiously divided, but would stem from the life of wheresoever it was practiced. This is as much as to talk about community. Yet this in turn must not be confused with 'community politics' as it is now practised, for that sort of politics takes the State as given and operates (frenetically) with whatever is left over from it: whereas a politics of meaning must precisely question the State itself—that is, the Nation State, which is the given of our political life—as the creature, *par excellence*, of the politics of knowledge.

A politics of meaning, in other words, is essentially constitutional. It must be concerned with those structures most propitious for a Green world. But this does not imply that, within some newly achieved structures, the old politics of getting and spending can be resumed. Rather, it implies that the constitutional process itself must become the continuing stuff of politics.

Such a process is simply one of putting things in their right and proper order: it is therefore a politics of which an aesthetic sense is at the heart. This virtually proposes itself, then, as a politics of place. To comprehend the connections of things, after all, is the prerogative of place, of local life. Now, in Britain it is one of our grander self-delusions that we have local government. We have no such thing. We have, rather, certain largely disconnected agencies of the State, subsumed under the titles of ancient earldoms revived about a hundred years ago for the purpose, once again, of serving the Crown's administration. As the inherent contradictions of the Nation State have mounted, however, so has that institution had to keep control of these agencies by using the one instrument that supplies its ultimate rationale: an instrument (of course) of measurement—namely, money. And so the hollowness at the political heart of local life becomes more and more exposed. In the result, all Britain has to show is the inexcusable and brutal ugliness of its cities, empty even of self-sustaining life: cities in which men have been snared in pursuit of their appetites for gain, and which now can only be abandoned to dereliction.

Perhaps this seems like a council of despair? If so, I would first say that it is one of the greatest diservices we do ourselves to suppose—no doubt, out of the mechanistic cast of our minds—that all social problems are somehow soluble. We are learning better in this respect, fortunately, but we still have a long way to go to arrive at the stark truth. Secondly, and alas! in all realism, more is likely to result from the crude collapse of the old way of life than from any depiction of the new. Surely, then, we shall live to see the dissolution of the Ministries!—for, by and large, they no longer believe in themselves. However, I can also see all manner of hope springing up around us: whether from the growth of local 'amenity' societies (but, one wonders, do these latter ever pause to question the source of their own inadequacy?) to signs that the citizens of Glasgow are beginning to take their city back from its commissars.

So what is all-important, I suggest, is that we keep our sense of direction: and the direction of Green politics is local life—together, conversely, with the end of the Nation State as we know it. Hence, participation in the politics of the Nation State should only be, not wantonly to disrupt it—for how could one excuse the compounding of misery?—but to take away its powers as they bear on local life. Above all, it should not be to patch up that State itself, for it is fundamentally flawed. So there is a role here for Greens of all parties: to engineer an abdication of the authority of the State as we know it, and so contrive another of those quiet English revolutions of which so much of our history has fortunately been composed.

All this may seem far from the environment—or, say, from whales, or co-operation rather than competitive business, or other ostensibly Green causes. If so, then I suggest this is only symptomatic of how far dependent we have become upon 'them' at the centre of politics to do things for us. It is this dependence, this very centre, that is the source of our problems: of the loss of control—responsibility, indeed—that underlies environmental pollution, etc, and that bespeaks the extraordinary centralization of affairs in Britain. (How synonymous this centralization has been with our national decline!) The 'environment', taken all in all, is nothing but the recovery of control over our own lives. What we do with that control, however, is the next question.

One is talking, in basic terms, of the replacement of the Nation by the Local State. This is not to propose the political restoration (or invention) of a whole set of small nations. The Nation State itself was largely a function of common language, as that language increasingly became the vehicle of the power of 'knowledge', The technology that accompanied this development will not go away, and where its scale is commensurate with the difference between one Nation State and another—that is, pre-eminently in the area of 'defence'—no doubt our present institutions must remain. But this technology and this power have dragged in their wake all manner of functions that belong to the small scale of life, and it is against this deprivation that the rebellion of the Local State must occur.

However, this is to speak but of the semblance of change. If the Nation State is bound somehow to persist, it must do so, not so much in parallel with the Local State—though confederate forms might become more common—but as a tolerated anachronism to a changed cast of our minds. (Incidentally, it is the attempt of the Green movement to live with the Nation State that largely accounts for its inner confusions. The Nation State is the political expression of a dualistic cast of mind, and all its disjunctions are inimical to ecology. The shiboleth of 'democracy', atomistic in concept as it is, is merely what has made the scale of the Nation State tolerable.) The cast of mind, then, concomitant with local political life is radically different from that which now dominates our politics. The passions governing the future will be quite other than those to which we now give priority.

Whilst the dominant values of a dualistic culture are ethical, of good and evil (for these predicate the distinctiveness of persons from the world), the predominant value of an ecological society is what is harmonious, seemingly 'of good report' (for this concerns belonging). This, in short, indicates the chasm to be crossed if our civilization is to continue. We shall have to learn to think qualitatively again, rather than quantitatively. Instead of 'growth' being the criterion of policy, appropriateness must be our concern. As well as rationality, we must admit intuition: inward knowledge (the gnostic) must balance outward. The feminine principle must play as much part in our affairs as the masculine. The processes of an ecological society are necessarily nondualistic (I shall not say 'holistic': that way lies the shadow of Hitler and Stalin); and this dictates a balance between the person and the world that only the structures of local life could accommodate. Constitutionally, we must know and be known, as now we cannot be.

The values of the old order have all but run their course. The structures built on them may end with a bang or a whimper—with a collapse of the credit structure of the Western world, or a slow disillusionment with materialism. Meantime, in this unreal kind of twilight, Green politics, lacking the structures in which it could flower, may seem in eclipse. But underneath, in the privacy of people's minds, the readiness for change is growing. We must make sure that when it comes it is well founded.

# GREENING OF SOCIALISM

Some of our friends are engaged in a rescue operation to save socialism from materialism. Yet can such an operation possibly succeed? The question is very important for the politics of the green movement as a whole—that movement which would unite the strands of an alternative to our current way of life in a new springtime of the imagination. Does brotherhood in fact somehow underlie the apparent indifference nowadays of one group of workers to the wellbeing of the whole, as socialism has always proclaimed? Or is it, as Jim Callaghan has recently discovered, that we are all acquisitive now? This is as much as to ask whether the Labour Party can be transformed from within, or whether the course of British politics can only be changed from outside the present structure.

It is in this context that it is pertinent to ask why nuclear power has hitherto had the almost unqualified support of the organized labour movement in this country. The answer lies in the remark of Frank Chapple, the EEPTU boss, quoted here: 'We have no choice but to use growth to help us solve our problems.' Dave Elliott's book* does a masterly job in exposing this grand illusion of our times, that nuclear power is in fact the key to continuous growth, and it is worth reading on those grounds alone. But this is quite a different matter from questioning whether growth itself is a desideratum of socialism.

* *The Politics of Nuclear Power*, Dave Elliott and others, London 1978

What concerns Dave Elliott and his co-authors is that nuclear power might be rejected as a result of the efforts of 'apolitical environmentalists' and that capitalism might then continue under an alternative 'technical fix'. To prevent this happening he seeks to persuade his fellow socialists that 'If we accept that a future socialist economy is merely a change in ownership of capitalist-spawned productive apparatus, we are not honestly confronting the basic contradictions of the capitalist political economy'. Technology is therefore not neutral, and a socialist society cannot be established simply by developing the techincal base developed within capitalism.

Anyone setting out to establish such notions must find themselves under a heavy weight of proof. (They are also entitled to much sympathy, as attempting to re-discover the supposedly 'lost idealism' of socialism.) For socialism has been about distribution: its effectiveness has lain in just such a context, and not a few of our present perplexities are due to the discovery that a measure of egalitarianism has done but little to solve our problems. Our expectations have if anything grown even further beyond our means of fulfilling them. Nothing has been said by the leaders of socialism to suggest that it would not be desirable always to have more to distribute. And technology, with nuclear power as its ultimate expression, has simply been accepted as the talisman of 'more': that is, of inducing nature to supply the very wants her prolixity squeezes up within us. If all this is no longer to be taken for granted, then, there are more assumptions to be questioned than this book in fact dreams of.

Consider the contradictions of technology, of which perhaps the major one is that in order to grow rich we become more alienated, the less ourselves! We develop large-scale, impersonal organizations and we suffer structural unemployment. Yet is not all this development fertile ground for the establishment of a working class, and sympathetic indeed to the very logic of socialism? For does not socialism treat of the person as a worker: a unit of the productive machine, of a class that exists objectively: as an object therefore? It is right to suggest, as this book does, that ownership—even the co-operatives seen by some as the last hope of a reconcillation of these contradictions—will change nothing so long as our technology is inherently alienating. Yet should work some-how recover its intrinsic value—as, that is, something worth doing for the meaning it has for the person who does it—it is at least probable that the bonds of proletariat solidarity would not be tightened thereby. And at most, it is probable that the only losers in such a process would be those who think about society in terms of class and in whose ideology there is no room for actual people.

In other words, the question has to be faced, whether the contradictions of technology are not also the contradictions of socialism as we know it, if only because socialism is in effect merely a function of capitalism? If this is so, socialism is sim-ply not free to discuss alternative technology. To do so would be tantamount to losing the loyalty of the working class and to failing it as the instrument of improvement of its standard of living. The grounds for thinking this in this case are undoubtedly strong, and they ultimately rest on the under-standing that socialism is as much based upon a quantitative, rather than a qualitative, view of the world as is capitalism. It should hardly be surprising were this so, indeed, for the com-mon ground of our historical epoch is, surely, the sanctity of knowledge, and what can be measured is what we think we know. Descartes set our forefathers upon the pursuit of cer-tainty with his concern for how he could be certain of what he knew and they followed him, perhaps less because of his argu-ment, than because they wished to overturn the arbitary powers of princes. We are living with the resultant knowledge explosion and its numerate rationality.

But we are also living, praise be! at the moment when this epoch is being questioned at its roots. That is to say, the paramouncy of knowledge is being questioned, if only because we can now see to what it leads: to an atomic holocaust, perhaps, and certainly to the despoilation of the world. Descartes had no qualms in saying that his ultimate purpose was to make mankind 'the Lords and Masters of Nature'. To us, that aim (much though we may sympathise with it against a background of life that was, indeed, 'nasty, brutish and short') becomes daily more suspect. For us, nowadays, it matters more and more what it means to know something.

At this point, it might be instructive to recall how New-ton spent ten years in what now seems like a desperate pursuit of alchemy. Probably, like Leibnitz, he held Descartes in con-tempt. Yet he must have felt the ground taken away from under him. His lesser successors succumbed, in any case, and accepted Descartes' clockwork universe with his conviction that God could not deceive us. Thus rational idealism became the cast of men's minds: a pre-conception of reality, and its explanations by means of a rational reduction of its parts. We still live under this thrall when it comes to our ideas about society. Our clockwork, perfectionist utopias and the ideologies that are their instruments still dominate our politics. They reduce people to things and count them up in order to demonstrate the certainty of the truths to be pro-nounced. And we submit to this, because knowledge is incon-trovertible and to know something it must be measured, and monetary value, after all, must be the social property of objects.

Yet, inexorably, the central concern of our lives today is shifting from knowledge to meaning. This is not only true of philosophy itself, it is also the only way in which the contem-porary alternative movement is comprehensible and it underlies the loss of confidence in, and the scepticism about, yesterday's certainties and its panaceas. We are beginning to sense that knowledge has made our expectations of the natural world illimitable, and that this must be an illusion. The sad thing is that socialism is caught up in this great climacteric. For socialism has been central to the idealism that was the guiding star of our lives; to renounce it must be very difficult. And what is being spoken of today as the shift of paradigm we are experiencing, is a shift from nothing less than idealism itself as a means of making sense of the world.

The shift from knowledge to meaning calls in question, of course, the central importance of measurability itself. A scepticism about statistical proof is anyway widespread by now. Of more significance, perhaps, a shift of emphasis towards intuitive perception, and hence towards the feminine rather than the masculine view of life, is in process. (This raises the question, how feminine is socialism?) The significance of this charge lies in the weight attaching to the whole, rather than the parts: to the shape, pattern, quality of a thing, rather than the measurable parts of which it is composed. We are beginning to feel a concern for the wood rather than the trees.

The danger in this situation, of the death of idealism, is that something more like national socialism, rather than socialism itself, will fill the vacuum. The nihilistic energy of facism was by no means quashed by the Hitler war. It seems to lie within our civilisation, alas! and has been expressed as much in our art as in the vandalism in our cities. This energy is at root maybe that of meaningless knowledge: of reaction against knowledge pursued for its own sake under the empty cloak of idealism. Be that as it may, the lost idealism of socialism is for us a dangerous condition in which to exist and should not be left to be filled by any rehashed variant.

This makes it important to say that an alternative politics is at least possible. It would be a politics about the forms of life—the new *cogitos*—of our future: the life-styles, communities, environments, the patterns of settlement, that cannot ultimately be explained, but the qualities of which can passionately be argued about. Such a politics would be as much about intangibles like identity—and hence about the urban/rural balance and the qualities of cities—as about private wealth (of which it would surely treat, but not in isolation from the places in which it was located). Such a politics would not partake of the fallacy of the late Tony Crosland's ladder—the ladder which he contended the middle-class environmentalists were trying to pull up behind them—for it would deal with more than just what is measurable. It would also be a politics in which places became the determinants, not the mere residues, of the technologies we employed—whether of education, with its apparatus of 'subjects' into which knowledge is supposedly divided, dictating schools of a certain size and hence communities of sorts; or of medicine, with its closure of hospitals on a human scale in the interests of its latest machines; or of transport, or of sewerage, or of energy—or anything else. It would be a politics in which people had a place, not ideologies. It might even be the long-lost politics of fraternity. And, it would be a politics in which all that matters about socialism would surely play its part.

This must be so, because the springhead of socialism is compassion for the deprived and concern for those whom society has unjustly treated. It is not those motivations that are in question, but the theoretical superstructure that rational idealism has erected upon them. This issue is coming to a head, because as the contradictions inherent in our knowledge-driven life-style become more acute, increasingly only the theory of socialism seems constant, held together as it is by its own logic; and so ideology and ideologues rule and our politics become ever more extreme. What alternative, then, can be offered to the energies of idealism that have generated this deformity and produced the familiar syndrome of the intellectual whose love of mankind is only sustained by his hatred of actual people?

It is for everyone concerned to discover their own solution to this problem. There are socialists who contend that socialism *is* ecology—the worlds of men and nature all comprehended in one system—and that therefore there is no need for any change in the political scene. In a sense they are all too right, and there are also ecologists who think that ecology is the new certainty, the new determinism, and that there is only one (ecological) answer to any question. In fact, however, there is room for many points of view, just as for many temperaments, within an ecological perspective—a perspective that starts with the whole rather than the parts of any social form, with its qualities rather than its quantities. There is an energy of everyday things upon which a 'green' politics must count: the energy that makes a reality of communities—rather, say, than partaking of the unreality of local government today, with its politics determined by sectoral, functional boundaries. In such a 'green' politics, there is room for argument about which are the realities that matter most, just as in many countries in Africa and Asia the village is given priority over the city. And there is room for compassion, because the unjust city is cruel to the poor. There is even scope for socialism to belie its name and be concerned for the natural environment, for if we are to live with Nature, not master it, our relationship to it must become personal again—based, as Martin Buber had it, on the 'I-Thou' word, not the 'I-It'—and there is nothing in such a relationship that is actually inimical to socialism. But whether, when all this happens, it would still be called 'socialism'—that is another (and, for some, perhaps, poignant) question.

What is interesting is whether Britain is not closer than we realize to this new kind of politics. The conventional view of this country is that it has lost its way: that it has no guiding purpose any more. (Or, alternatively, that we are merely unsuccessful materialists, rationalising our failures.) But perhaps the crisis is really in the minds of those who think only in idealistic categories. Maybe the sickness is in them. Britain arguably has tasted materialism in both its garbs, and spat it out. Its concern could lie, rather, with the manifold forms life takes, all its great variety, not with some one purpose, for which a crusade might be made. If this proved to be the case, it would after all be nothing but this country discovering once again that the only wealth is life.

# CHAPTER THREE

# Philosophy
# of Wholeness

# Philosophy of Wholeness

## A GREEN THOUGHT IN A GREEN SHADE

The Green Movement has been in search of a philosophy, though it's by no means certain, not just whether it has found one, but whether it would recognize it if it had. I do not say this necessarily to discourage the pursuit of some philosophical underpinning to the new paradigm comparable to Descartes' underpinning of the old, but rather because the case is different. Indeed, I would say the trouble with the old paradigm is precisely that it was philosophically underpinned. As a result, we are left with a spiritual vacuum. I do not think it follows, however, that what is needed is an 'eco-theology' to match some eco-philosophy, so much as the elimination of the distinction—indeed, the gulf immemorially taken for granted by the West—between philosophy and theology themselves. Our ever-increasing concern for the environment, in other words, may be a catalyst of far deeper consequence than not only those politicians adopting a green tinge, but philosophers also, yet realize.

To be concerned for the environment is to acknowledge that the causal relationships we comprehend do not comprehend all that is to be comprehended about the cause and effect of which they treat. And yet, what else do we comprehend? We comprehend the fragments into which, following Descartes' advice—but, really, only following the logic of the

West's presumption about the atomistic structure of the world, stemming (all too significantly) from Democritus— the fragments, then, into which we must reduce the world if we wish to control it.

That such knowledge, such an epistomology, could ever be given credence (and Newton and Leibnitz, let it be remembered, were amongst those who did not credit it) could only be because it issued from an unchallengeable authority about some over-riding Providence. Indeed, Descartes remained faithful to his Jesuit superiors. 'God would not deceive us', he said about the logical vacuum he posited between the Self and the world. The erosion of this faith amongst his successors, then, is surely accountable only by the power over the world which Descartes' method has given us, as indeed he intended it should. He intended . . . yet could see no harm in that, for was not mankind God's surrogate on this earth? If so, it is doubt about how we have used that power that is now asking questions of the sanction that first gave us command of it.

Of course, the 'science' of ecology has stepped into the breach as the respectable agent within the old epistomology to explain the manifold effects of any given cause. Its efforts and achievements are benign, in that they have drawn attention to a much wider field of effects of any application of our knowledge than has hitherto been the case. Ecology's ultimate limitation, however, it that it does not question that knowledge itself; or rather, it has nothing to say about its meaning. After all, no one could say we are wise in our time, and it is our wisdom, not our knowledge, that is now in question.

Indeed, we do not just lack wisdom in the conduct of our affairs; our lives have reached a pitch of meaninglessness—of which drug addiction, vandalism, etc. are but the outward signs—empty of all but materialism, and which threatens the stability of our society. For society doesn't work, even in its own terms—any more than Imperial Rome, that other great forcing ground of a new faith, came to work in its own terms. And though materialism is not to be despised—matter and mother (mater), after all, come from the same root—nor to be displaced by pure spirit, any more than the sun could be replaced by the moon, yet even science itself is now telling us that much, and perhaps all, we thought of as matter is in fact relationship: is relationships of relationships.

Now, prima facie, 'the environment' is everything, all things taken together, rather than nothing. Or is it, rather, everything bar something? Well, to speak is to speak of something and so to not speak of something else; just as to speak of everything would be to not speak at all. Our speech is founded in the grammar of subject and object, in dualism, therefore, both of the Self and the world and of the separateness of all things that are not other things—all to the extent that the tongues of different nations may bewitch them by their descriptive potential. So, if the environment is everything, rather than just another object, does it not take us to the bounds of speech?

To pose this question is to suggest some affinity of the environment with God. For, note, the notion of God is inherent in language. As every parent soon discovers, it is not long before the very young child learns the question 'Why?' The ultimate impossibility of answering this question as the child, in what is a sort of religious act, pursues it, lies less in our lack of knowledge than in the incapacity of language, tied as it is to the grammar of dualism, to satisfy the need it has itself aroused.

When we come to the point where the question of how things happen turns into the question of why they happen, the separate compartments of grammar lack the connectedness to do anything but resort to God. I do not mean, conventionally speaking, that we invent God—though God may take many forms, wear different clothes—but that God is inherent to speech. It requires an extreme sophistication, one beyond the Western mentality, hobbled as it is by the separation of philosophy from theology, to suppose other-wise: that is, to conceive that God is not necessarily to be brought into the world, and personalized. For the West, however, he is the First Cause, only the origin of which is inscrutible to us. The essential particularity of language has thus led us to where only generality—the divine—can make sense if we want to keep talking at all.

So, at the least, the environment, if understood as all things taken together, carries intimations of the spiritual, of what is holy. This is also as much as to say that our concern for it marks the restoration of a spiritual dimension to our lives. There is indeed a mysterious core to the notion of the environment. There is, for sure, a language for each of its parts, but what binds these languages we cannot say. (Is it perhaps the fear that if we did not share these languages amongst ourselves, they would each have but little gram-mar—and hence there would be no common language worth having?) This is not to imply that nothing can be said about the environment: only, rather, that what can be said lies beyond the bounds of dualistic speech, and therefore is in the realm of the poetic, and of the qualititive and the allusive, rather than the quantitative and the analytic. But it is also to suggest that it carries no necessary implication of God.

Now, religion is about the Great Doubt (to use Buddhist terminology): that is its matrix. This is far from the doubt of Descartes, the fallacy—indeed, the littleness—of which was long ago exposed by David Hume (but whose exposure was at the time too inconvenient to be taken to heart by the prevalent peddlers of the power of 'knowledge'). The Great Doubt, then, is not about whether we exist, but whether our existence—its joys, as much as its sorrows, but especially its sorrows—has any meaning.

Meaning, I take it, lies in the conformation to some pattern by whatsoever it is that the meaning is in question. Hence, if 'the environment' is indeed all things taken together, its meaning, as Wittgenstein said of the world itself, is outside the world. But this is not to say that 'God' is the meaning of the world, for 'he' is a function of language, which is of the world. Indeed, were God outside the world, he would be meaningless to the world and personally arbitrary so far as its conformity to any pattern was concerned.

Such reasons, no doubt, are what lie behind the alternative assumption so many people make about 'the environment': namely, that it is, rather, everything that is not something, and is therefore just another object. As such, people may claim 'the environment' as theirs—as, for instance, people protected by some Green Belt are prone to do. No doubt such a position is tenable, but it carries with it the handicap, not to say the stigma, of treating of something by reductive thought that can be reduced to nothing but its possessibility. Rather, surely, the challenge is to face the other alternative: that 'the environment' is the totality of things.

In sum, we are evidently here close to that notion of God which perhaps commands the most profound respect: the notion of God beyond God. This is what caused Meister Eckhart to say, 'I flee from God for the sake of God', and likewise, it is from this that the Zen adage, 'If you meet the Buddha on the way, kill him' derives. And so do the Godhead, Brahma, and other such respectable notions of God beyond God the Creator. Thus, our contemporary concern for the environment—imposed as it is by the disastrous consequences of our atomism—poses religious questions, questions about meaning and reality—which cannot be shelved if humanity is to avoid suicide.

Inescapably amongst those questions is that of the Self. It is raised in a new and heightened form by the very notion of the environment. For the Self, in the dualistic paradigm, stands in contrast to and apart from all the immensity of the world and its multiplicity; it is that which is within, the autonomously directed Person. If, however, the environment is not susceptible to being understood from within the dualistic paradigm, it must enclose the 'Self' in reciprocity with the world. This, of course, bears upon what Theodore Roszak has termed the Person-Planet relationship and, if the environment is indeed not just another object, it bespeaks a breakdown in the subject-object relationship which underlies the very grammar of language. Perhaps, then, it may be surmised that the planet is implicate in the person but, be that as it may, the question brings into play the differing concepts of Man held by the great religions.

In so far, then, as 'the environment' belies causation—is comprehensible only as a totality, as what it is—the very notion of it strikes at the roots of reductionistic thought. And what are those roots? They can only lie in an ontology which separates God from Man. For then reality, all that is, is God's domain, which Man cannot enter: from which, indeed, he has been expelled. Man is he who can only know in part: who, because he knows anything, cannot know everything, and therefore can never embrace reality. This is not to say that were there no God, Man might be all knowing. But it is to say that what Man might know, his notion of reality, would then be different. The irony is, in fact, that in such a case it is 'reality' itself (not God) that would be mysterious.

Obviously enough, then, the challenge of the environment, if understood as being anachronistic to dualistic thought, is to nothing less than Christianity itself: or rather, perhaps, to the materialism that has left Christianity high and dry as the spiritual tide has (inevitably) flowed away from it. Conversely, the mystery that must always lie at the core of the environment if, and in so far as, that concept paradigmatically conforms to the changing relationship of observer and observed, and as it thus bespeaks a breakdown of dualism, would readily consort with, say, the philosophic/ theological Buddhist notion of 'nothingness' (sunyata).

There need be nothing surprising about such a conclusion, thus far. The connections between industrial society and Christianity have long since been described from many angles, just as the connections between industrialism and environmental concern are obvious. One cannot leave matters there, however, for they are not so clear-cut. Japan, for one thing, has shown that a people with its roots in Buddhism—a non-individualistic people, and one for whom the notion of profit is immoral—can adapt to industrialism and subject itself to pollution in so doing. Furthermore, no matter how flawed it might be, it would be unthinkable for the West to renounce the whole culture of Christendom. We should be a people without a history, and left demented thereby. Because the old paradigm has produced such philosophically deformed monstrosities as modern economics, or because our politics are sterile (and they are premised only on the entirely dispensable concept of the Nation State) it does not follow that all should be flushed away: not Chartres, or even the Romantics, say, or my village church. Besides, there is a new ontology, a new sense of the real, emerging.

I say this with the more conviction because the adoption of Buddhism by the West at the expense of Christianity (if that fantasy may be allowed) would not of itself resolve matters for us. It would not do so because Buddhism and Christianity, it seems to me, share a flaw in common.

Buddism, for all its sophistication—which stems from its having recognized that language presumes God, and that therefore God is not a sufficient premise for any ontology (which all gives it a certain affinity with Western existentialism)—Buddhism, then, yet shares with the West the assumption that language describes reality. (The great Madhyamika philosopher, Nagarjuna, as well as Dogen, the great Zen master, and perhaps other strands of Zen, must be accounted exceptions to this.) I wonder if it is not this that has led (as it has led the European Existentialists) not merely into some convoluted uses of language, but into an introverted concern with the Self—with the losing of it, of course, rather than, as with Christians, the finding of it—which underlies the accusation of quietism against Buddhism and its emphasis on the monastic life?

The thinking behind this speculation is that despite the Mahayanan (Greater Vehicle) refutation, two thousand years ago, of the human atomism of Hiniyanan (Lesser Vehicle) Buddhism, and its replacement by their perception that all is but process, I think it is by no means clear that Buddhist practice has escaped from the presumption that words describe the reality of the world. Consequently, Buddhism remains haunted by the hard fact of life and death: it has not escaped from the bewitchment of our unique possession of language. Ultimately, it seems to me, even 'nothingness' is something: 'emptiness is form' indeed. At all events, this continuing dependence upon description of a thing as a thing may help account for the vulnerability of Buddhist countries to environmental pollution—a much more difficult phenomenon to grasp, I think, than their adoption of industrialism itself. Such dependence can only give more importance to the trees than the wood, or even to the words than the poem.

Now, the emergent ontology I have mentioned breaks with this commonly held connection between words and the world. Wittgenstein's aphorism 'the meaning of a word is its use in the language' is perhaps the best summary of this ontology—or rather, the best introduction to the resultant labyrinth in our pursuit of the real. What it ultimately amounts to is that reality lies in what it is not an abuse of words to say—and that, it seems to me, is a kind of worship: an acceptance of the pathos of the word, and that it is holy.

To accept the world thus is to be part of it 'oneself'. It is to treat of the 'Self' as a sometimes necessary form of life: that is, something about which one's 'spade is turned' when at some time one has said all that can usefully be said—although at another time one might say more; one might 'place the books in a different order on the shelf.' This, essentially, is to treat observer and observed, subject and object, as one, and is how the environment must be given its due.

To give the environment its due, however, is not to invent a new religion; it is rather to pursue a new way of life—albeit a sacramental one. Nor is this so startling; it is already happening. It is happening, not least, in the industrial world, where people are asking for and are giving a meaningful say to work—for there is nothing incompatible, *per se*, between technology and the sacramental—though the connection of scale therewith may be closer. It is happening more slowly in political life, though, without constitutional change, matters cannot go much further there. Not surprisingly, it is not yet happening at all in education, for education exists to purvey knowledge and the knowledge that it knows is not of its own devising. But it will happen even there because the system is self-evidently bankrupt. Generally, however, in so far as 'the environment' serves to bring home to mankind that we live within a great mystery, we shall abate the arrogance with which we exercise our mastery over matter. (If, for instance, the 'greenhouse' effect produces anything like the flooding of great cities now in prospect we shall surely become more circumspect in our actions.) Briefly, then, to think in these terms is no more than to echo the poetry in Ecclesiasticus about the lives of humble, untutored craftsmen:

*All these put their trust in their hands;*
*And each becometh wise in his own work.*
*Without these shall not a city be inhabited,*
*And men shall not sojourn nor walk up and down therein.*
*They shall not be sought for in the council of the people,*
*And in the assembly they shall not mount on high;*
*They shall not sit on the seat of the judge,*
*And they shall not understand the covenant of judgement;*
*Neither shall they declare instruction and judgement;*
*And where parables are they shall not be found.*
*But they will maintain the fabric of the world;*
*And in the handywork of their craft is their prayer.*

I cannot think any temples would be built to a faith of this kind, though it need not lack for rituals of a spontaneous nature, grave as well as gay. After all, there are innumerable lay priests in our society today, though unrecognized as such, like doctors and scientists and schoolteachers, committed to a sublimation of the ego, and who propagate their mysteries and build their temples, such as hospitals and atom-smashing plants and soulless schools. The difference with a society of which the mystery of the environment lay at the core would be that, logically, its ethic would be one of play, of what is done for its own sake, not work, and the poetic would be its prime concern. Yet this is not to say that all other temples should be pulled down. Indeed, it is seriously to be considered whether in fact only hybrid faiths can ever satisfy mankind.

This possibility may seem remote, for there is a millenarian intolerance in 'Christianity' (there are, alas! many millenarians in the Green Movement) that would seem to preclude any such accommodation—an intolerance that to Islam makes of Christianity something merely esoteric, fit only for the monastery. ('No monkery in Islam,' said Mohammet.) Yet, until Nicea (AD 325), Christianity was undecided between the Athanasians (of the Trinity) and the Arians (of God undivided), and, with that event in the politics of Rome, it lost forever—and worse than lost: persecuted—its gnostic heart, and so irremediably personalized God through the Son. Is it impossible to suppose that Zen might fill this void and help Christianity to find itself again, and thus save the West from itself?

Were this to happen, it would be because Zen is practical, has its feet on the ground, yet understands the limits of conceptualization. ('Fire does not burn fire, and water does not wet water'.) This understanding marches with an innate respect for the environment as a mystery. The West, for its part, is redeemed by having itself become aware of the need for that respect; though within itself it has lost the means of satisfying it. Christianity, as Dostoievsky's Grand Inquisitor in effect told Christ returned to earth, at least satisfies the craving of the mind torn by dualism (and unable to face the rigours of non-duality, of mindfulness) for rest, for 'peace'. Conversely for Zen, in Japan, the animism of Shinto now provides but a frail partner in withstanding the pressures of today's materialism. Is some such new graft, then, entirely unrealistic? At least the Church is beginning to fill the vacuum in our society. May it only be clear that its old prescriptions will not suffice!

Personally, I think the West is worth saving. It is for Christians to say whether they will stoop to being rescued. If so, the environment is a catalyst waiting to be activated. In any case, it is from this spiritual resource that the power of the Green Movement stems.

# THE GRAMMAR OF GOD

To assume God is not to believe in God. Of such is the decadence of our secular society: for we hold to the constructs that stem from the assumption of God, but without any more believing in God. To accomplish this it is in fact only necessary to cling to a tenet, that the fragmented world we have contrived is providentially real, and hence, as by some hidden hand, will cohere—which is why the gathering ecological crisis is ultimately a threat to our sense of reality itself; so it is no wonder we are pervaded by foreboding, nor that any profound questioning of the Christianity in which we no longer believe is none the less as profoundly resented. Yet, in these circumstances, to call God in aid once again is less than constructive. For language itself hypothesizes God. 'In the beginning was the Word, and the Word was with God, and the Word was God.' But the Word is potentially both subject and object, the knower as well as the known. So it was that St. John promptly took the course of official Christianity through the mystique of the Word: 'The Word became flesh, and dwelt among us, full of grace and truth; we have beheld His glory, glory as of the only Son from the Father.'

By this personalization, the language of God was to be made intelligible to mankind, and our concepts about the known were to be transmitted through the power of authority. What language described could thus be nothing but real, and so we have conceived a reified world, a world of things, causally driven by millenarian forces towards salvation by God, from whom the grammar of language has but temporarily separated us. The Self likewise was reified—such that the search for it has continued through the Christian ages—for, as knowers of the known, if our knowing is not of reality now should we who know be real? Yet, none the less, there are civilizations, perhaps wiser than ours, whose philosophies recognize that no ontology, no notion of reality, can rest upon God, since God is a predicate of language itself, in which the word 'why' is embedded. The rest, alas! theologize.

In the West, in particular, with our hybrid heritage of monotheism (Jewish) and idealism (Greek), the odds were stacked against the gnostic strain that was there in early Christianity, which offered no certainty, no permanence. The exigencies of Roman politics prevailed over this. Whatsoever was said or written could thenceforth be taken to reflect only the immutable, the 'objective', concrete and absolute, for otherwise the reality of both the speaker and what was spoken of would be brought into question: and that would be to bring God into question. Yet in the East (perhaps not having Rome to contend with) they saw beyond all this reification—and so, two thousand years ago, civilisation forked between theism and non-theism. And even if in the West today the priests of its churches may not count for much, they have but been replaced by all the other priests—the scientists, doctors, economists—of the residual materialism of theism, of that reification to which theistic mystification ineluctably resorts. This is all the more so in the case of Christianity because of its trinitarianism. The trinity made the essential incomprehensibility of Creation susceptible to hierarchical authority, as all the persuasions of prophesy could not have done—but did so at the cost of dividing Man himself: of dualism, opposing mind to body, soul to matter, person to world, self to society.

Some now call for holism to bring this dualism to an end, because of the threat it is seen to pose to our survival in the world we have violated. Well, perhaps holism would be preferable to dualism, perhaps not: but it still presupposes the subject-object relationship of language—for the whole is still an object—so, logically, it is still theistic, and predicates a theistic society—as does Islam, for instance. (Or, in its degenerate secular form, it bespeaks Marxism, or Fascism.) For holism is not the same as non-dualism, which is the mode of speech whereby Buddhism would avoid our bewitchment by language. Yet, for the Western mentality, the implications of non-dualism seem bleakly negative: the only prescriptions it seems to offer are negative ones—of what should not be done—whilst the 'emptiness' of all concepts is the only reality. The glory of the world is thus not in what is true, but only in what is not false: hence, in what is —simply, in health, rather than in Heaven.

This recalls Wittgenstein's dictum, that 'philosophy leaves things as they are'. Wittgenstein, indeed, whose philosophy uncannily but unconsciously echoes Mahayanan Buddhist thought of two thousand years ago, being himself of the West, was very conscious of how much this was asking us to accept. The best he could suggest was that this Western craving for the absolute, to make things real, should merely be indulged in order that wisdom might grow from the resultant disillusion. Yet is it not just here that the significance of the ecological is to be found? For the ecological refers to interconnectedness, and thus sees wisdom in the everydayness of life, in what transpires from moment to moment, for it is in this that the multiplicity of events accumulates of which the universe is miraculouslly compounded. To be aware of this cannot be otherwise than to conceive of the world as holy. This being so, it must be our prime concern not to muck up the world by abusing our gift of language to promote the illusions of materialism, Yet to think of the world as holy it is in no way necessary to call God in aid.

However, whether God should none the less be called in aid is a different question: one to do with human frailty in face of a landscape too bleak to be borne by our seekers of Paradise, our speech-bewitched species. It is the question of whether it is practicable to suppose that civilization can be sustained without the trappings of some system of belief in all its materiality?

This was essentially the theme of Dostoievsky's great parable of the Grand Inquisitor (who, in compassion, had Christ burnt at the stake when he returned to earth and disturbed the people so). It is also raised by the question of whether Buddhism, which is not without its own concessions to human frailty, could have survived in Japan without the co-existence of animistic Shintoism, or of today's underculture of the 'water trade'; just as it is raised by what is to happen in Liverpool, or Brixton. And it suggests why the materialistic West still resists any alternative to the Christianity it has abandoned. Well, whether mankind is so frail or no, whether or no the ceremonies should be kept, what matters is that at least we should recognise we are frail: that we should not mistake our frailty—our materialism—for strength, as now we do in rejoicing in our dominion over the earth. Our work, it follows should become our play: at best a game, in which we confess we need to be indulged. What marvels, all around us and under our very noses, might we not then come to appreciate!

# CHAPTER FOUR

# *Wholeness in Planning*

# *Wholeness in Planning*

## THE DEATH OF IDEALISM

It is only with an effort that we can now recall now high were once the hopes of planning. Partly, this is because planning itself has by now become mundane: a part of the everyday grind. And partly it is because those hopes and all their energies have transferred themselves elsewhere: initially, to the environmental movement, latterly to ecology. It could be salutary, then, to recognize why all this has happened.

Planning (remember) was going to build a new world. From at least the 'thirties onwards till, say, the early 'sixties, planning was to be the instrument of those who stood back from day-to-day preoccupations to determine where we were going and to set the strategy of change. Nowadays, that kind of exercise is largely discredited, even though at the same time people lament the lack of any larger vision or of any sense of direction to our affairs.

This loss of credibility, however, is understandable. In practice, planning has become synonymous with bureaucracy and with resentment over its intrusion into every corner of our lives. In reaction, the voice of 'the people' has replaced the mandarins as the tell-tale of the winds of change. In its turn, however, this posture threatens at best to reduce the role of planners simply to one of reaction to others' initiatives: at worst, it could mean the abandonment of planning. In either case, any larger vision is the probable casualty.

This discussion has been couched so far in terms of planning at large. Land-use planning indeed suffers from the current opprobrium of planning in general, as well as from the blame heaped upon those mythical creatures 'the planners', for sins (such as high-rise flats) which were rather committed by the politicians, architects and, indeed, the media themselves, who in the mood of the times endorsed policies which actual planners were often the only people to oppose. Yet, in a sense, the thrust of the blame is reasonable enough, for what is under attack is the process associated with planning, whether as practiced by planners, politicians, architects, or the media at one remove.

Nevertheless, it should be realized that land-use planning is essentially not the same as, say, economic 'planning', or industrial 'planning'. The former really has a claim to the name, because the entities it treats of are different in kind from the latter. That is to say, whereas economic and political criteria provide the rationale of much that passes for 'planning', there are no other criteria for making order in towns and cities than those of planning itself.

What unifies all planning, however, is its concern for the wholeness of things: for seeing the whole of any thing, rather than the parts into which it might be reduced. And this concern is arguably a profound hunger in ourselves today, for we are governed by a mode of understanding that proceeds by atomisation: by reducing all things to their parts. (The fact that in sub-atomic physics we have reached a point where there are no 'things' anymore, only relationships, is but grist to my argument. It is the patterns and forms life takes that are indestructable, not their components.) That reductionism, for all the control it has given us over the world about us, does indeed leave a void in our experience is endorsed by the recognition by medical science, that with one hemisphere of the brain we actually do comprehend the forms of things, seeing them whole. It is this hemisphere (in fact, the right one) that has become atrophied in our culture, with the arts confined to their ghetto, and it is fair to surmise that it was because planning once promised to be the hand-maiden to this side of our nature that it briefly became so potent in our affairs.

This craving for wholeness in our lives (not in any mystical or universal sense, necessarily, but just to see the wood from the trees) has most commonly, perhaps, expressed itself in Utopias—the very notion of which, significantly enough, parallelled the emergence of rationalism. Is it not plausible, indeed, that Utopianism has been the fatal ingredient in the planning movement of our days? For reductionist thought and Utopianism are not opposites: on the contrary. After all, rational idealism has been the governing philosophy of our civilization ever since the pursuit of certainty began to dominate men's minds in the seventeeth century. Idealism, indeed, has since the Greeks, in one form or another been, in Wittgenstein's phrase, the spectacles through which we see the world and which we never take off the ends of our noses. Science itself has long since come to terms with it through the medium of the clockwork universe. Scientism has thus been the instrument of our ideological Utopias, whether of Marx or Hitler.

The primacy we accord knowledge, the criterion of measurement (and hence of whatsoever is measurable) with which we are supplied to justify whatever we do (together with the greed for 'more' that we have institutionalized), prescribes a detailed oversight of everybody's life in any Utopia. An ideal society cannot be flawed in any detail. Idealism is thus the seed-bed of bureaucracy—and this perhaps explains the irony in our times, namely of its all being so well-meant. Furthermore, knowledge is inherently hier-archical; the distillation by which it is pursued conduces naturally to some centre where it is kept. By and large, alas! Whitehall does know best. Likewise, knowledge is power, and bigness—and, also, alienation.

Aye, there's the rub! This, the sense of depersonal-

ization, of the inhumanity at the heart of all our arrangements, of people being used as objects, is what is day by day
giving pause to the chariot on which our civilization has
hitherto progressed. When people speak, as they now do, of
the paradigm shift through which we are living, it is to all this
alienation that they refer. It is meaning, not knowledge,
which is becoming central to philosophy. And the real
question is not whether it is just rational idealism and its way
of understanding the world that is being discarded, as surely it
is, but idealism itself—those spectacles we never take off. For
the indissouluble dichotomy of 'person' and 'world'—of the
soul and the universe—goes back (in the West) to the origins
of Christianity itself: to the questions of God and Caesar. And
what is argued by our condition today is that, after two
thousand years, those solutions have not worked, and we
must go back to the beginnings.

It should not be surprising, perhaps, that with all this
luggage to carry, planning should have failed as the
instrument of an ideal new world. Yet it should also be
realised that planning was first appropriated by, and to, the
old paradigm; it was itself bureaucratized, for instance, before
the bureaucracy became so suspect. Overtly, this happened in
Britain primarily because within a very few years of the
passing of the great Planning Act of 1947 the means had been
taken away from planners of implementing their plans. The
financial provisions of the Act were repealed in 1954, and
from that moment onwards planning became immersed in an
administrative machine, and its practice a matter merely of
unlimited technicalities. There were ideological considerations behind that repeal, naturally, concerning who got what
out of this new-fangled eccentricity of 'planning'. But much
more fundamentally, planning to politicians of all parties
must, with its queer rules of propriety, have been sensed as a
profound threat to the regular conduct of life—as witness the
fact, for instance, that the (Labour) government of the day
quite undisguisedly adopted the New Towns programme only

as an expedient provision of housing.

And, indeed, planning was—and is—just such a threat, more profound, alas! than even the planners have understood. For what implicitly was being said by planning, then as now, was that the whole comes before the parts. And this remains truly radical, because in practice it means that all our technologies should be subordinate to the forms of our settlements—to our towns, villages, cities, regions. But in the event, (the implementation of planning having been emasculated) planners have perforce drawn up their plans such that the several technologies—of education, health, housing, water, transport, commerce, industry—determined the places where we lived, and local government itself lost its opportunity to become something more significant than a stitched-up collection of agencies, with power within it deployed along functional lines—making, say,the Education Committee a little law unto itself—and not for the community.

Alas! the torch which planning dropped was in the 'sixties picked up on behalf of the environment. 'Alas!' because the supposed whole which 'the environment' represented was in fact very partial. It more or less excluded mankind: or, at least, it assumed a certain given social status quo—which again had its ideological overtones. Yet the passionate dynamic of the environmental movement was all too understandable; for the very primacy of knowledge, to which planning in its turn had become subordinate, was beginning to pose implacable threats to the natural world. Indeed, had not Descartes' very purpose been to make us 'the Lords and Masters of Nature'? Yet would not Nature, as always, have the last laugh? Would we not be wise, then, to respect it, rather than to master it?

This was all obviously true, but the so partial nature of environmentalism, its blindness to Man, was equally patent. The vacuum this left—one which, for instance, the UN 'Habitat' Conference in Vancouver sought (but failed) to fill, in the aftermath of the Environment Conference in

Stockholm—is one the ecological movement has more recently sought to occupy. For ecologists, an ecological system involves Man and Nature impartially—and this is a great advance. Yet, at bottom, the ecology movement has no more renounced certainty as our prime concern than have the other ideologies of the day. For it, not only is the ecological viewpoint the right one, but there is only one ecological viewpoint possible. There is a tinge of authoritarianism in this, which observers have not failed to detect, and which threatens to turn ecology into just one more fad. After all, Hitler dwelt upon such worthy objects as 'the community': an essential concept, but one which is only now recovering from the bad name he and his like gave it. So we must surely outgrow organicism, and this is perhaps the contribution planning has to make to the alliance of forces now gathering around the shift of paradigm.

Should we not, then, assess planning again? For planning is not (what it has become) something just to be endured as part of life's importunities. Rather, it is a different way of seeing the world; it is actually the greatest force for change lying practically to hand—all the more so because it does not treat of the grandiose, but of the forms of everyday life. To say something as simple, as that form should determine function—that the town should condition the kind of schooling it provides, say, or the health services it contains—is nevertheless to turn our present world upside-down. Yet planning is about just such simplicities. No ideology is at issue in this. We are dealing with everyday realities, so ordinary that nobody seems to notice them. Planning is about making places, and places encompass all of human life: you cannot be unconcerned even with social justice, say, if you are concerned with a place—but if social justice is your sole concern you will never make a place that encompasses all of human life. To make (and remake) the places where we live, which is the vocation of planning, and to provide an identity by so doing, is to treat of forms rather than functions, and of meaning rather than knowledge. The validity of planning, thus construed, remains as powerful as it ever was.

But there are no linguistic cosmetics for disguising the meaning that 'planning' has acquired. The problem is not to think up some trendy new word for an old activity. The problem, rather, is to find practical ways of at last making that activity effective. And the key to this, surely, lies in the actual implementation of plans—that part of planning which so quickly fell into disuse after the 1947 Act. Hence, the question is one of development agencies; and, politically, the reality to be faced is that local authorities as we know them are not constituted to be such agencies, because they are structured to operate along, not across, functional lines. Therefore the problem to be solved is one of devising agencies that can work with (not supplant) local authorities as they are. And this should not be an impossible problem to solve—basically, because we shall thereby have foresworn Utopianism and its predeliction to organize everything and to plan every detail of our lives. Planning actually only needs to be structural. Yet if this shift did come about, it would not be surprising to find that statutory authorities became increasingly satisfied to delegate their powers—especially, say, in education and health—to effective local bodies which sprang out of the forms by which we live, and cut the tendrils of the centre. Planners should begin to assert the role of communities as determinants of technology: of what knowledge means. Then we should not need Utopias.

# THE DISSOLUTION OF THE MINISTRIES

In these hard times, how ironic it would be if the disrepute into which planning has fallen were to drag the Town and Country Planning Association down with it! The Association, after all, was founded at the turn of the century by someone, Ebenezer Howard, who was not a planner: someone, moreover, who had conceived of 'a peaceful path to real reform' such as is unrecognizable in the activities of any Planning Authority in the land today: and for years it has warned planners themselves of the need to put their house in order. Yet in the public mind the TCPA has become inseparable from the planning system.

Perhaps it is not only in the public mind that this is the case. The Association itself changed its name, and incorporated the word 'planning' into its title, back in 1919. An ambiguous relationship with the profession persists. There is to be sure much common ground. This consists in a concern for wholeness. Howard's Garden City, like his Social City, was conceived as a whole: the whole determined the parts, which made no sense except in terms of the whole. Likewise, planners are distinguished by their concern, not with the merits of any proposal in itself, but with how it accords with some form of things: whether of a town as a whole, or a region, or a street. The wholeness is what matters. And since our lives are too dominated by a contrary concern—by a concern for the technical properties of matter reduced to its particulars—to have a champion of wholeness in the arena of public life has seemed invaluable. Yet, alas! something has gone wrong with planning. Its vision has seemed to extort too great a cost. It is important to understand why.

Planning, in fact, has become synonymous with the Them and Us syndrome against which there has been such revulsion. This does not reflect wholeness, but its opposite. It bespeaks dualism. As such, then, it is no more than the conventional mode of our thought: the mode upon which our mechanistic idea of the universe is founded and by which we have sought to master Nature. That is, in dualistic thought observer is separated from observed, as mind is from body, or the person from the world, or the spiritual from the material. This is the paradigm or pattern of ideas, governing the way we in the West make sense of life, including our society. We associate it above all with Descartes' separation of the Self, as a 'thinking substance', from the world, and all the rational idealism that resulted therefrom in the conception of Creation as a great machine.

Thus, Hobbes created his Leviathan, the progenitor of the Nation State, from Galileo's ideas of motion: Man was a restless creature, whose 'natural state was Warre,' and who must be tamed by the power of the centre. And Jefferson, in writing the veritable proclamation of democracy, was paradigmatically equating the natural rights of Man with Newton's force of gravity. The arts, not least, have partaken of this paradigm, with the separation of the artist from the world, just as the frame isolates the canvas. Planning, then, even in its pursuit of wholeness, merely accepted this scheme (of planner and planned) as inherent to its practice. Hence, if the revulsion against planning is particularly strong—and revulsion is, of course, widespread, affecting all the professions and the political system at large—it is perhaps because planning seemed to promise something otherwise. The disillusion is with its pretence of wholeness.

The rock upon which our pattern of life has been founded is the dualistic idea of knowledge: that is, what the observer knows about what is observed. This is what the Nation
State itself is founded upon, for as Francis Bacon pronounced at the outset of the Enlightenment: 'Knowledge itself is
power'. Of what, then, do we have this knowledge? We have it
of the things of which the world is composed: of the building-
blocks of matter, to the reduction of which all our skill is
employed. People themselves are but some of these building-
blocks. The State, to draw this knowledge into its hands, has
rarefied (jargonized) language, and simultaneously stretched
power to the boundaries of each common tongue. (The
Nation State, one might say, is the politicization of language.)
Its bureaucracy controls the specialisms into which the
corpus of knowledge is broken down. A necessary expedient
of that bureaucracy, then, as its managing agent, became
Local Government, which was ruthlessly compartment-
alized to provide the services the State had it in its power to
dispense.

Of course, 'Local Government' held resonances of
another kind of world—of another paradigm, even. It
romantically called to mind a world of neighbours in which
the measurement of things was not dominant and in which
'wealth' had connotations outside the calculus of money: a
world, above all, in which the knowledge of things held no
precedence over the meaning of that knowledge. This
ambivalence has no doubt led, at this very moment of crisis,
to the Government's dilemma: that is, as to whether the
Secretary of State should heed his heart or his head over
Local Government—or, alternatively, whether inner or outer
knowledge should be heeded. Nevertheless, the logic of
knowledge as power is inexorable. Local Government is
nowadays increasingly revealed as the fraud it is: an
administrative convenience that is a parody both of government and of what is local. At all costs, it seems, if our kind of
society is not to fall apart, its values must be measured; and

money, in its discrete, reducible units, is what counts. What is serious, then, is not so much that those romantic resonances of Local Government are now being sacrificed in the interests of the State–it was always fated that they would be— but that we shall be left in the desert of a quantitative world.

What this quantitative world has offered above all—its very seduction—is certainty. With this insurance we have pursued the politics of GNP and 'growth' and the way of life of the consumer society. The temptation for planning to professionalize itself, therefore, like all the rest, and so to join the mainstream, has been understandable and irresistible. Planners, too, have wanted to offer Us the goods we need. They have become technicians, creating products in the form of end-state conditions. The cost of it all, however, and the source of the reaction against it, has been the treatment of people as objects, deterministically serving the causes and effects of social engineering.

For planners, the retribution people are now exercising upon those impersonal forces that would seek to govern society is especially severe because the 'goods' provided by planning are nothing if not whole forms of life. The denial which this constitutes of personal identity seems so much the greater than that which any particular technology could exercise. Thus ironically, by becoming professionalized, planning has come to represent the whole of the impersonal structure of society.

These points, abstruse as they may be, must be made because there should be no delusions about how deep are the changes needed. To speak of 'decentralisation,' say, or 'participation' as sovereign remedies for the sickness of planning is ultimately facile. Planning has allowed itself to become part of the paradigm still governing our minds, and is paying the penalty for it. The State invented Local Government, of which planning is a part—and what the State giveth, it taketh away. As the difficulties of the State multiply—as the alienations of the idea of knowledge upon which it is founded express themselves in inflation, unemployment, resource depletion and indebtedness—so it must tighten its control, or disintegrate.

It is sad, if inevitable, that planning has allowed itself to be but one more creature of the State. Ebenezer Howard, however, when he conceived of the 'Garden City' did not set out to invent just another tool for the armoury of the State. On the contrary, he wrote (and acted) at a time when, significantly, he must have seen the State—faced with the growing miseries of the formless industrial cities—at the beginning of the process which by now has robbed local life of meaning. He wanted the nation, rather, to take a different path altogether. When, instead, it proceeded on its course of idealistic centralization, planning was perhaps bound to be incorporated into the machine, where its essential wholeness could only be an anachronism. What place in the machine is there for the intuitive, the qualitative, the feminine, those attributes of wholeness? How can one speak of wholes when communities are replaced by 'catchment areas'? Now that centralism can be seen to have run its course, however, what is to be done? What can be saved?

The question is not really, what should be done about planning, but what should we as citizens, as members of communities, do? For, if the foregoing analysis is roughly correct, there is nothing planning can do about itself. It, 'planning,' is trapped in its context—a change in which alone could make any significant difference, yet which planning itself is clearly powerless to effect. The paradigm itself, no less, must shift: the very pattern of our thoughts, such that the way we think about planning is changed along with how we make sense of the world at large.

And, of course, the paradigm is shifting. The mechanistic universe from which all our metaphors derive has been demolished by Quantum Mechanics. Certainty has been replaced by uncertainty as the habitation of our minds.

So, just as observer and observed can no more be separated, the planner apart from the planned no longer carries any conviction, and the certitudes which They conveyed to Us no longer have creditability. Reality itself is not about things, but consists in process, and, in place of determinism, there is an oscillation to be conceived between the person and the world. After all, the arts for their part have already presaged this shift, with their discrediting of the art object. Remember the Tate's pile of bricks?

Of course, if we were just dealing with notions in the mind, none of this would matter very much. But, in fact, we are dealing, if not with reality (whatever that actually is), then with a 'language-game': namely, the ceaseless interplay between words and the world, between ideas and what happens. And what is happening is the breakdown of our simplistic view of the world: of the wages economy, in which supply equalled demand (for what?), and jobs were one and the same as work. We have thoroughly exploited the world—and lost our moral being in so doing. We are left with its fragments, yet, for all we know of them, they offer us no meaning. Alienation, in the midst of plenty, is the last fruit of dualism. Our cities, which were the product of rampaging dualism—and of its essentially short-term accounting—are now the detritus of its decline. No one believes in Utopia any more.

This is a world that no longer works. Perhaps, then, it is no wonder that our thoughts turn from a world of things, atoms, to one of process. If in society the only sign of this shift is the, by now, ineradicable contempt in which politics is held, this is surely because it strikes at the heart of the system by which we live: the Nation State itself. This it does because the shift is from knowledge—that concept from which (in no matter what pseudo disguise) central political power descends—to meaning. For process, in contradistinction to the knowledge we have of things, is intelligible only in terms of patterns, shapes, forms; and these are notions which confer meaning, rather than knowledge, upon their components. So, if meaning is once again to become the driving force of society—if, for instance, appropriate technology (to borrow from Schumacher) rather than technology for its own sake, is to be espoused as a tenet of life—the Local State must supersede the Nation State. This is simply because, the more local is life, the more meaningful it must be.

These are, of course, revolutionary notions—and revolution, though hopefully a peaceful one, there certainly will be. (Of course, this revolution has nothing to do with egalitarianism, which is merely a function of reductionist thought. How do you measure environmental wealth?) The 'Peaceful path to real reform' can only be pursued—as was always, esentially, what the Garden City was about—by the localisation of life, for only in that way can wholeness be practised. The person has to see what his presence in the world means, and in seeing he changes it. Technology is what has hitherto determined scale. For the person to determine technology, and hence scale, would be a revolution more deep-seated than anything conventionally 'political'.

In this revolution, the central part will be played by whatever it is that sees 'the pattern that connects,' in Bateson's term. I doubt if this could be 'planning' as we know it. Maybe, however, it could be Buddhist planning. An absurdity? Well, Fritz Schumacher wrote a famous essay—now a chapter in *Small is Beautiful*—on 'Buddhist Economics'. In it he showed that commodities—their getting and spending—were not the only rationale for an economy. Similarly, if not product but process were the rationale of planning—not what kind of towns should be made, but how—it would be logical to call such planning 'Buddhist', for to Buddhists reality consists not in things but in process. If the process of planning, however, is to pursue a pattern that connects—if, that is, it is to hold any meaning—it must take place within forms that allow this to happen.

Perhaps this comes close to saying that 'planning' could become superfluous if only we got the contexts of our lives right. It could indeed be argued that planning has evolved only in compensation for the disintegration of local life— somehow to substitute for its lost appearances. To the extent this is true, it is the elimination of the causes of that disintegration, rather than an enhancement of the appearances— as when commuters replace the indigenous inhabitants of a village—that is called for. In other words if communities existed in any meaningful way, their 'planning' could be dispensed with. The question is thus not so much the restitution of planning as it is a constitutional one. Where should the power over our lives lie?

The solution to this question has to do with the replacement of the Nation State by the Local State. One could speak of the dissolution of the Ministries, for the chains of centralisation must be broken. It would be fitting for the TCPA to embark upon such a campaign, for Ebenezer Howard foresaw new forms of life arising: forms activated, not by the power of the State and professional knowledge, but by the resources that their own development would generate. Form would determine function: the community, for instance, might be the school. As it is, of course, we are in thrall to the centre—no matter that the education system itself has clearly come to the end of its road, and seems more meaningless every day. Yet, how can one seriously speak of breaking this spell?

Well, imagine a country in which one third of all public money is expended by parish councils, another third by the counties and only the last third by the State itself! Moreover, in this imaginary country it is the local councils (the commons) which decide upon what the State shall be allowed to spend money. And, should some issue arise which spans local boundaries, the local authorities concerned (not the State) will determine whether some *ad hoc* body shall be established to deal with it. Such a country, you might say, would be inconceivable, given the realities of power in the Nation State—and you would probably be right. Yet just such a country exists in the midst of the Western world—and arguably does so precisely because it alone is not, by the normal criteria; a Nation State: That is to say, this particular country has not stretched political power to the boundaries of a common tongue, and no common tongue has been used there for the spread of knowledge as an instrument of power. The country in question, of course, is Switzerland—so, for 'parishes' read 'communes' or 'gemeinde,' for 'counties' read 'cantons,' and for the ad hoc solution of common problems read 'regional planning.' This country, then, serves as a standing example that we do not have to be governed as we are, from the top down. Nor, surely, is it entirely coincidental that Switzerland for long has had the West's lowest inflation rate: when public expenditure is local, after all, money actually has meaning—and then perhaps even 'monetarism' works. Oh! and incidentally, Switzerland (that poor unenlightened country) seems to manage without a Ministry of Education.

So the campaign to be fought is not just for a flacid policy of decentralization. Decentralization merely increases the power of deciding what shall or shall not be decentralized. The centre, rather, must abdicate. ALL POWER TO THE LOCALITY might be our slogan. The centre is hollow, anyway, and suffering from a massive loss of self-confidence. Its only weapon is money, and in its heart it now knows how little money solves, including the problems of the inner cities— those monuments to the quantitative society. (The solution to that problem lies in their qualitative transformation, which the power structure of the Nation State—the clout of the old cities against the centre—has hitherto stood in the way of.) This is not to say that local authorities as we have them are the right bodies to which to transfer power. They are conceived as service agencies, lacking wholeness. (That is why Development Corporations, with their concern for some place or other as a whole, are in certain senses acceptable.) But they would be our natural allies at the start of any campaign.

Planning—the fly in the ointment of Local Government as we know it: the one discipline to see things whole—could become the agent of this revolution. But only planning which sees itself as process: the process of people making the places with which they wish to identify themselves: grass-roots planning, in colloquial terms; which means a pulse passing between people and the world, annihilating dualism, creating wholes, in which technology is servant, not master. And if that sort of planning could not see how a local Development Land Tax would provide its most important source of independent finance—far more so than local income tax—it would need its brains testing.

The objection to this scenario from those of the mandarin mentality—the 'educated classes'—will be: 'parochialism'! But we live in a world of communications—not least, of the 'box'—such as nullifies parochialism. Never, since the Church provided the common ground of a civilization for those who lived all their lives in villages, has there been so much for mankind to share. 'Think globally, act locally' is merely common-sense advice. Acting locally, however, is still the missing component, because the centre does it all for us. That is what the TCPA should campaign to change. In changing it, it would coincidentally be helping an historically new kind of person to evolve.

# WHY WINDSCALE ?

What on earth is a responsible body like the Town and Country Planning Association doing, involving itself with the Windscale Inquiry? All very well, perhaps, to want to see fair play, and therefore to have urged the Inquiry itself. A matter so lethal as the production of plutonium by reprocessing nuclear waste should not, as a question of common sense, go by default—or, if not by default, by decision beyond the normal competence of some local planning committee. But, that objective won (as it has been), what competence has the Association itself beyond that of any planning committee?

The answer lies in the story that started seventy years ago, and more. At the turn of the century, the garden cities movement, in an essentially modest way, set out on a path of peaceful reform. It did not announce some ideology, as subsequently our political parties have done, and therefore it did not influence or recruit the intelligentsia of the country. What it offered, rather, was a balance between intelligence and feeling, just as it proposed a balance between town and country. Between the squalid industrial city and a stagnant countryside it offered, in Howard's diagram of the magnets— that veritable logo of planning—an alternative which struck a chord in the minds of those many who have distrusted the ideological abstractions which now govern our political lives. This alternative, then, was fundamantally ecological: that is to say, it took for granted the natural systems of life on which it was posited, and it considered mankind as part of that totality. The green belts that surrounded Howard's garden cities were agricultural in kind (rather than just recreational, as they have since essentially become) and yielded up the fruits of the earth in conjunction with the products of the city.

The only thing was, thenceforth we took Nature for granted. It was perhaps inevitable we should have done so. All our intelligence favours that idea. Nature, after all, is that upon which we exercise our wits. We bend our minds to extract from the world about us whatsoever it can offer. Ever since Descartes declared that he existed because he thought ('I concluded that I was a substance whose whole essence or nature consists in thinking'), the natural world has stood apart from ourselves, and we have only needed to lay our rule across it and so discover its laws in order to master it. Our expectations of it have become limitless. This was our arrogance: the hubris that now threatens our destruction.

Yet, if the garden cities movement itself also took Nature for granted, it could surely be excused! What man had done to man in the course of the Industrial Revolution was outrageous. For men had treated one another as objects, as parts of that very external world which Descartes specified. Society and social considerations therefore rightly became central to the Association's activities, as also its strength. Whilst others defended or attacked the social *status quo* behind the given forms of human settlement, whether of the industrial city or the feudal countryside, the Association kept its eye unfailingly on the social realities of those forms. Whilst architectural fashions and intellectual fads came and went— and, for instance, high rise solutions to the maladies of the city were tried, and in all humanity found wanting—the Association grew in stature by the simple prescription of concern for what it means for Everyman to be living in a city today.

So we took Nature's side of the equation for granted.

Indeed, we implicity welcomed the exploitation of the earth's resources, because the era of cheap energy did more to fire the process of dispersal from the overcrowded cities than all our preaching had done. (That this dispersal, thus fired, overwhelmingly took a mean form, aggraviating the alien-ations of industrialism by the spread of suburbs, doesn't alter the present case.) It is for this reason that the TCPA has been reluctant to join in with the environmental lobby of recent years. Stockholm was a jamboree for those concerned for Nature but not for Man. Indeed, it often seemed as if their prescription for Man was to squeeze him back into the cities and leave him there to stew. 'Habitat', in Vancouver, was meant to rectify this balance, but proved a fiasco in its own terms; ideologies held the stage, because the diplomats had not grasped the positive side of planning's simple rationale: that, by taking thought and appropriating the values of development (and only those values), we can make the places where we live.

In the aftermath of that fiasco it was necessary to take stock. The failure of planning—of those who want to make villages or cities—to penetrate the consciousness of the world stood in contrast to those who want to rescue Nature from Man. Moreover, these two groups simply did not understand each other's language. A city, for instance, means something very different (and old-fashioned) to the environmentalists from what it now means to planners; and, as for new towns, they conjure up entirely different meanings. Conversely, the makers of cities have been prone to accept the one-eyed commercial rationalisation of, say, the extinction of the sperm whale, or the use of pesticides; for the environ-mentalists, however, these acts have quite different meanings. It is the issue of nuclear energy that, in the end, has brought these different languages together.

Planners, it is probably fair to say, have hitherto wanted nuclear power, and that means plutonium power, to arrive. It seemed to guarantee the realisation of their dreams and to conform to their acceptance of Man as the thinking animal, always one step ahead of Nature. What is now giving them pause for thought, however, is not whether plutonium power can be produced—whether Man's technology is capable of coming to the rescue in an energy famine—but whether it ought to be produced. This is not, of course, a question limited to planners. But it is of unusual concern to planners, in that the way the question is asked, the kind of question it is, is in principle the same as is asked of planners in their business of making cities, villages and towns. The question, that is, is not one of quantities, but of qualities: not whether the thing can be done—because it can be measured, either in scientific or monetary terms—but what meaning there would be in the doing.

In other words, Windscale is about our minds, and of what they are composed. The making of plutonium risks doing violence to both Nature and Man. And the risks are such that they are beyond computation, because if the violence occurred the process would be irreversible: the position could never be restored. In an instant, then, this changes the centre of our being. That centre, these several hundred years, has been to do with knowledge. Today, accordingly, we inhabit the Cartesian paradigm, the universe as Descartes understood it, and central to that paradigm is what we know and how we know it. It is this very cast of mind that could now do irreversible violence to both Nature and Man.

Thus, if the question Windscale poses is that of a plutonium economy, as it is, then the alternative is not just of a reduced standard of living without the aid of limitless energy; rather, it is of a change in the very concept of a standard of living, and therewith of all the values we now hold. A non-plutonium world would be a post-Cartesian world. The very idea that Nature is there for its secrets to be unlocked and exploited for our use would be exchanged for an idea of interdependence between Man and Nature. And one of the most immediate changes in our values would concern those assumptions which have allowed British Nuclear Fuels Limited to be established with a commercial remit. A more dangerous temptation to cut the corners of our civilization could not be imagined. Yet because we value measurement in itself—and money seems to measure the social properties of objects—we allow such madness. None of this is to decry science—Descartes' approach must never be confused with Newton's—but only to draw attention to the attitudes we must bring to science. It is always salutary to remember how the Chinese refrained from putting gunpowder to military use.

As for planning, it can be said that it was never to its purpose to build the good city at lasting cost to the natural world. That such would be the case in a plutonium society there can hardly be any doubt. The challenge to planning, therefore, is to show that there are forms of human settlement that could sustain a non-plutonium society. The development of such forms is the contribution planning has to make to the new values governing such a world. That this challenge can be met is the ultimate reason why the human dimension must be represented in any inquiry into the making of plutonium out of nuclear waste at Windscale.

# AFTER SCHUMACHER

An ironic transmutation has occurred. That champion of nuclear power, the Central Electricity Board, was to be heard at the gigantic Sizewell Inquiry justifying its economic case on grounds of an exponential rise in energy costs, reminiscent of the Club of Rome's arguments of more than ten years back and also, at but one remove, of Schumacher's; whereas the objectors to nuclear power found themselves discounting the myth of any 'energy crisis' at all.

The price of oil, Peter Odell argued, was set to fall for the foreseeable future and (all virtually regardless of political vagaries) its consumption only modestly to rise compared with the post-war decades. The world has at least the same thirty year oil future before it that it had the day before the first Arab oil embargo.

We have, in brief, lived through an entirely artificial period in the oil market; and what Man makes Man can, and in some measure most probably will, undo. After all, the stuff can be got out of the ground in Saudi Arabia at $5 a barrel, and at $7 even in the North Sea. Moreover, world consumption has been falling over the past ten years—at a rate of 0.6% per annum. No wonder the pound sterling, oil currency that it is, has become so tender! In 'collapse conditions', indeed, the price of oil could even revert to basic 1970 levels. Interestingly, then, Paul Hawkins, a persuasive advocate of alternative economics, also says in his book *The Next Economy* that there is no 'energy crisis', conventionally speaking, nor is the next economy contingent thereon.

Schumacher himself poured scorn on the Club of Rome's general concern for the depletion of all the world's finite resources. (See Schumacher's *Small is Beautiful,* Chapter 8.) For him—with a perhaps uncharacteristic linearity of vision—the whole issue of depletion could be reduced to the factor of energy. To the extent, therefore, that others have followed him in this thinking, he would have to bear some responsibility for the failure of this supposed touchstone of the New Age.

At the same time, Schumacher's warnings have, quite naturally and properly, had their effect upon the conservation and the more responsible use of energy, which itself has played a large part in the subsequent turn of events—and this discounting of his prediction is something of which the true prophet in him would surely have approved. One can say this the more certainly because nothing in it detracts from Schumacher's basic polemic, that we cannot indefinitely count the world's capital as our income.

Or can we? Indeed, the danger is that we shall now let out the baby with the bath water. Highly sophisticated technology (as well as much of it on the low, or common sense, level) has made a major contribution to the saving of energy. We have arguably been creating capital in our store of knowledge about energy control as fast as we have been using up the world. Nature's last laugh has thus been postponed, perhaps (almost) indefinitely. Yet Schumacher, in all conscience, had so much more than this to say; and that there has been a concentration on his preaching about energy is a consequence of nothing less than the divided inheritance he left.

Or rather, truth to tell, it is we who have divided his inheritance. The division rests in ourselves, and is bound to do so, no matter what we inherit, or from whom. It lies between the material and the spiritual, or between body and mind—call it what you will. Schumacher subsumed both sides of this typically Western divide in himself and in his practice: that is what singles him out. But, being the kind of society ours is, it was the material aspect of this message that was popularized. The exhaustion of the world's energies some may have thought would simply frighten us into being good. Yet Schumacher's whole message, because it really did not distinguish between the material and the spiritual, was far more difficult to grasp. And the use of advanced technology to prolong the availablility of fossil fuels—unobjectionable as that surely might seem—actually serves to bring that message all the more acutely home.

This message asks of us, what is energy for? This is a question that will not sink back again into obscurity once the immediate danger is past of our being without the supply of energy to which we have become accustomed. It will not do so, because the cure of that shortage both confirms and even further aggravates the deeper unease to which our exploitation of energy has brought us.

The more we focus our concern on energy for its own sake, in other words, the more we shall be fixed in the meaninglessness of that position. The manifestation of this meaninglessness is in the disjunctures of our society—disjunctures which the plenitude of energy has increasingly licensed us to create. And this is as much as to say that the disconnections of our society—not least the now commonplace separation of the employed from the unemployed—will only worsen by reason of this saving of energy.

Schumacher, to be sure, inveighed ceaselessly against our profligacy with Nature, warning us above all to conserve our resources of coal. (It was a tragically lost opportunity that the last coal strike was fought, not on the grounds of common interest in the conservation of coal—as Schumacher would have urged—but on the kind of selfish grounds we all too understandably recognize. As ever, those whom the gods destroy...) Yet Schumacher did not preach just that we should be more 'economic' in our use of resources; indeed, as in Buddhist Economics, he questioned economics itself at its roots. Rather, he rejected the whole paradigm of thought that underlies our exploitation of the natural world. Nowhere is this more clear (nor less remarked upon within the Alternative Movement) than in 'The Party's Over,' the last chapter of Good Work. Such talk as is to be found there of the balefulness of Cartesianism is, perhaps, less easy to assimilate than some Apocalypse caused by the using up of our sources of energy. But we shall none the less have to learn that vocabulary.

So Schumacher was not talking, ultimately, in terms of capital and income at all, no matter how these might be re-defined. What concerned him, I suggest, was that in both making and using capital we should be separating ourselves— as Descartes affirmed we, as thinking substances, are separate—from the objects of our thought.

Of this separation, the consequences ensue—far more immediately and acutely than just in any shortage of energy—in the disjunctures of our society. And, of course, it was to these that Schumacher began to turn in the last two chapters of *Small is Beautiful*, dwelling therein upon putative co-operative structures of business. In truth, the 'energy crisis' of the 'Seventies was virtually a distraction (or at most a portent) from the failures of our society to fit together: failures which any merely technical solution of the energy crisis will only further aggravate. Our irresponsible depletion of the world has been but a special case of our lost wholeness.

Other cases of this loss, after all, are now manifold. Technology has taken charge (because we have let it do so), fragmenting all in its path. It permeates the precarious balance of nuclear terror; the instability of the world's credit system, with its illusions of meeting its huge indebtedness; the mismatch of the job market; the dereliction of cities; the growth of crime as a way of life; the polarization of North and South; pollution; that devaluation of relationships we call 'inflation'; the remorseless centralization of power, and so on: what does it not permeate? These disjunctures of the world will more than suffice to keep alive the question, what is energy for: energy, the so casual use of which has in one way and another brought them all upon us, no matter how plentiful it remains? For, regardless of how hard they strive, all the King's horses and all the King's civil servants cannot put Humpty Dumpty—our distracted society—together again.

Now, the matter cannot be left there. If resource depletion is a simplistic explanation of our woes, it is only reasonable to demand a deeper, a more arduous, examination. It is not knowledge, after all, we lack, or for want of which the world is all out of joint. Rather, surely, that knowledge has created a vacuum of meaning. Our practices are subordinate only to the rescripts of their technologies. It is the sheer meaninglessness of those practices, the nihilism endemic in the West, that has set us adrift, without bearings. And it is the replacement of knowledge by the primacy of meaning, concealed under the innocuous term of 'appropriate technology,' that signals—this, rather than any new technology of itself—the profound changes we associate with Schumacher.

Yet—and this is where the Green movement must still logically be prepared to follow—this is as much as to challenge our most prized characteristic: our individualism. Our individualism—as Locke caused it to be enshrined in the Bill of Rights, the virtual British Constitution—is but one side of a coin of which the other is the Nation State, the Leviathan wherewith Hobbes sought to tame the natural restlessness of mankind. For our individualism derives from the kind of knowledge we have cultivated. As individuals—and hence as units, or particles, of the social entities to which we belong—we each have some special knowledge, and therefore some particular power through the roles we play in the world, and this knowledge is such that the knower of it stands apart therefrom: and so he plays his part. Thus, to challenge the primacy of knowledge and subordinate it to meaning (if knowledge, that is, must rather conform to some pattern of its use) is to challenge the modern State itself.

Put in another way, the 'energy crisis' has only concealed a constitutional crisis: it is a crisis of the governability of an individualistic society. So we are talking now, perforce, of the Local State—which means, the displacement of the current farce of 'local government'—and of the dissolution of the Ministries. This is the real transmutation now in process.

We must talk in this way because it is not of individuals but of people we must treat if we wish to inhabit a coherent world. People are not units, not one part of a duality with society, but autonomous and each with an inner and an outer life. Yet person can connect with person; for I can feel your pain, can I not, and you can sense that I do so? Imagination is the handmaid of meaning—just as 'alienation' is the cry of despair of the individual in the trap of dualistic knowledge.In any case, for sure, we share the language of pain—and language is all the observance we have.

In Western culture, however, the community this connectedness presumes has atrophied, shrunk to something very small. In Japan, conversely by example, they may have their 'wa', their sence of national harmony; and hence, perhaps, the Japanese are not individuals, but they are people, and so better able than ourselves to withstand the divisiveness of technology. With our different history, however, it is only on the small scale that we can now expect life to hold together again: the scale on which person can still be known to person.

This is not to advocate the abolition af all the nation states of Europe (and elsewhere) and their replacement by mini-states. For one thing, the technology of warfare cannot be dis-invented and will remain appropriate to the states we have; and for another, there are disjunctures of industrialism, particularly pollution, that can be dealt with only on the large scale. However, those manifold strongholds of functionalism from which Government is now exercised could be broken—and broken to the great enrichment of local life.

This is perhaps not the place to develop the point, for it bears upon the details of the shackles of centrally imposed standards—whether in school curricula, fire services, building, etc. etc.—and their replacement by locally determined criteria. However, it needs to be said here that if it be questioned whether a locality of such and such a size can supply such and such a (functionally determined) service, and hence concluded that the catchment area of sevices generally must be the determinant of 'government', then let it be answered that community, not catchment area, should be the determinant of function if meaning, not knowledge, is to be the regulator of the constitution!

And if it be objected that community nowadays is at odds with functional desiderata—of water, police, education, housing, transport, planning, health, etc.—then let the contrary be proclaimed: that the whole is still implicate in the parts! In other words, that in the most local community (which is all that is left to our fragmented culture) the seed is still perceptible of the constitution as a whole, of the State itself. That is, you cannot find yourself in, say, Solihull, or Liverpool 8, or Hartland, and not know of what you also find yourself a part. From this premise it follows, then, that the greater entity is subordinate to the smaller, for therein meaning resides. The State is implicate in the parish—or, more nearly, the commune, or Gemeinde.

We have travelled a long way, then, from the falling price of oil—let alone from the recent huge, world-wide discoveries of cheap coal—and equally far from the popular image of Schumacher as the simple prophet of doom. Yet the first Arab oil embargo was a convulsion after which nothing could be the same. It exposes the vacuum at the centre of all our certainties. In so doing, indeed, it has perhaps prepared the ground all too well for the religious revivalism by which it now sometimes seems we are beset.

Instead, I think it is the inner stillness we shall have to investigate. It needs to be commonly known, for instance, that Newton nearly killed himself with mercury poisoning, after ten years of secret alchemical experiments, because he saw there was no meaning in the mechanistic universe he himself presaged. (When we understand that Newton himself did not conceive of the mechanical universe, we may become wise.) Rather than any dearth of resources, it is the language animal, Man himself, that we need to be frightened of, for by his abuse of words, his scientistic abstractions, he destroys meaning. As Schumacher said, we have to make the statistics sing—and, to do that ,we must inhabit forms of life that would lend them meaning.

# PLANNING, GROWTH—AND CHANGE

Now is the time to make a statement of faith. As we all pull in our belts, as the country's aspirations contract, it is easy to assume there can be no more developments: hence, no future to plan for. Post-war planning, we are told, though we did not know it, has been dependent on growth; whilst the Minister for Local Government and Planning himself (John Silkin) is reported to have said that, whilst this economic climate lasts, new towns have but a low claim on public expenditure. Yet, in fact, such statements only reflect the very frame of mind—the essential conservatism—that has brought us to our present pass. Let the convinced planners, therefore, now stand up and be counted!

Planning, as the Town and Country Planning Association understands it, was never the creature of growth: we never presumed this condition. Rather, planning was based on change: change, essentially, in different conditions of land tenure. Of course, to have ignored economic growth would have been politically problematic; and in the result neither our overcrowded cities nor our emergent city regions were well served by the form it took. Yet even well into the epoch of post-war planning, the policy of dispersal never presumed growth. It would be distressing to think we have been seduced into depending upon it, forgetting the principles which in their own right justified that policy. It is easy to see, indeed, how the passive acceptance of developers' initiatives could have lulled planning into this frame of mind, as the planning system has slowly degenerated over the last twenty years. The real importance of the Community Land Act may be precisely that it could alter this frame of mind.

Put alternatively, are we now so satisfied with our cities? Undoubtedly, the overcrowding which first motivated the policy of planned dispersal is much reduced. The old London, for instance—what we now call Inner London—has been losing population at an average rate of 50,000 a year since 1930; and ironically, the average was as high in the pre-war years as since. From Greater London as a whole, the latest estimates suggest, the outflow amounts to about 100,000 per annum, of which only a small proportion is going to planned town expansions. As things are, this sum may or may not lessen, but the point is rather, that with housing obsolescence now rising at the gallop predicted by the Greater London Development Plan, but with the Plan itself moribund, the boroughs still perversely seek to rehouse people in schemes at densities clearly intolerable to them. It is salutary to remember Ebenezer Howard's contention, around the turn of the century, 'that the present area of the London County Council ought not . . . to contain more than, say, one-fifth of its present population'. He substantiated the claim in detail; it is his vision, however, we need to recapture.

It is not the physical quantity of land, but its value (which, within any city, has been rising for faster than the population has been leaving) that has been determining the exodus. In this light, then, there is no solution in sight to the problems of space—not of crude physical usage, but of urban social geometry—within the city itself. This is as true of low-rise high-density solutions as of discredited high-rise itself, despite the fashionable advocates of London's Lillington Street, who ignore its unrepeatable costs. (Go and observe the decline of standards in that scheme, from the impossibly expensive first phase to the mundane third and last!) And the more the post-war solutions have been pursued, the greater the mess to be cleared up. Alas! we have made rods for our own backs—or rather, the once fashionable arrogance of 'urbanity' has done so—for generations to come. It is not growth we need for our motive power, but greater compassion.

Yet just as planning and growth are not synonymous, is not a profound shift of values taking place? Even without growth, there can be no question of returning to the past, too many recent changes, surely, are irreversible. We have had a taste of other things; our minds have been unshackled. To live with one's mother-in-law, for instance, can no longer be accepted as the norm: in other words, the fragmentation of families now has deep-seated social causes, not just financial ones. And the obsolescence of Britain's housing stock is such that these pressures to make new households will enforce continuous development and redevelopment upon us.

Nor should we make any easy assumptions about the ground-swell of change. We assume too naturally that current changes in our social relationships are but the consequences of economic growth. It could as likely be the other way around: in particular, the reasons for the present economic decline must lie in deeper social causes and, greatest of all ironies, lie even in the spread of that education on which so many hopes have been placed. The movement towards equality of the sexes, as just one instance, with all its structural social implications (including the emergent symmetrical family) is not likely to be reversed as incomes fall. Likewise, what might be termed the flight from alienation will not halt with any decline in growth, and may well have precipitated it: that is, the rejection by people, in their millions, of all the impersonality of large-scale production; the apparent bloody-mindedness of educated workers whose jobs carry no meaning for their lives, except the pay packet. (It could hardly be claimed, surely, that the rationalization of the production line remains as the idealization of work it once was.) Of course, so long as materialism pays off it may maintain its dominance. What we are witnessing, however, is a major reinforcement of the doubts about its even paying off.

Maybe planning is not philosophy, though I think it is. But in so far as its practice lies in those areas precisely outside the activities in which we are so sure of ourselves, planning is bound to be apart from our ruling ideas. At present, those very ideas are in question. That this is the case—that two fundamentally different philosophies, or ways of wanting to understand the world, are in conflict—is suggested by the failure of the present system to work as it should. Thus, we are experiencing unemployment with inflation, or rising prices with falling demand—things undreamt of in neo-Keynsian philosophy. The great post-war spread of education, after all, has created a commensurate rise in expectations. Alas! the idea of knowledge on which that education is based is of a mechanistic universe, the fruits of which we need only the keys of science and mathematics to unlock. Consequently its possibilities seem limitless, justifying our expectations of what the world owes us. Yet whether this rape of nature has any meaning for our lives, or whether society can be perfectly institutionalized without the destruction of all personality, is precisely the doubt now spreading. We may here particularly question whether one manifestation of our alienations—that is, violence as a way of urban life—is much longer acceptable.

To cast our ideas in these terms, then, is to think about qualities, not quantities; and quality is the very currency of planning. ('Growth' is the least of essentials to it.) Planning is practised because the market with its quantitative measures cannot satisfy all our needs. (Planning does not, of course, deny the market.) Planning's own rationale lies in the discussion conducted in Britain amongst a close group of people, a kind of intelligentsia of aesthetes, whether architects or publicists, and administrators with a classical education, but in whose discourse the bystanders have now lost confidence. It is now up to the rest of us, therefore, to speak up in human terms about the places where we live. So (if there is truth in this analysis of the changes afoot) the role planning should play must be greater, not less than in the past.

Indeed, our cities face a huge restructuring if any sense is to be made of them in contemporary terms. So long as the home-centred family retains its influence, cities will have to be redesigned to accommodate it. It is almost as simple as that. The mere rehabilitation of old urban areas is as much of an illusion, in this respect, as was their former demolition and reconstruction. Alone, it will solve nothing. Yet these are the new blinkers our decision-takers are so gladly trying for size. It is urban structure, rather, they need to look at: and, for a start, questions of centrality and decentralization within the urban fabric itself. The world over, other cities are now doing this—consider Paris, or Moscow even—but in Britain there is only stagnation.

Our inhibition, whatever it is, is all too well illustrated by the burgeoning but futile controversy over new towns and the inner cities: the new towns-*versus*-inner city fallacy. These are not real alternatives. The only real alternative remains: planned or planless dispersal. Within the old cities themselves no socially acceptable solution, for all the wishful thinking of the city-as-it-was romantics, exists. The only question for those cities is, how shall they be restructured? The mystique of Corbusier having worn thin, revealing the sterility of life beneath its surface, not only has no urbanist ideal emerged to replace it—and certainly not futurism, or any such technological solution—but mere common sense disallows the possibility. At all costs, then, let us not retrace those steps of the discussion. Rather, let us build on the logic of dispersal, to make new cities with the urban qualities to which people will respond. This cannot be done, however, without changing their structures.

Perhaps our inhibition about this has been inherent in the very process of dispersal these last twenty years. Because it has been more by push than pull—that is, by the failure of cities to satisfy our aspirations, rather than the attraction of other centres of life—the process has benefited the least inert: the young and the better off, the footloose. And the cities, futilely treating their own symptoms, not the underlying causes, have aggravated matters by creating huge pools of immobility: the (effectively) tied populations of public housing tenants, creating the servile city. New York should stand as a dreadful warning of the welfare city solution—of making life worse for the weak by actually sustaining their hostile environment—rather than a solution by planning: that is, by restructuring the city region itself. It is, after all, the cities' wealth, not their poverty, that has brought their problems upon them. The lesson, surely, is to mobilize the poor and to agree the practical possibilities of doing this by developing new centres, whether in or beyond the urban fabric, within the reach of all. In this, only the cities can help themselves.

We shall doubtless hear much special pleading on this issue, if only because this would be consonant with the ruling assumptions of the closed circle that governs us. Thus we may expect to be told that heavy public investment in inner cities is necessary to attract more private investment there. What a huge trigger mechanism that would indeed need to be!—not only because of its heavy unit costs, but because inevitably it would all be wasted. Private investment would not turn its tide and follow public investment back into the inner cities, because the rising land values that initially drove it out would by this process be increased. The fact is that if some of our more rigid mentors could have their way we should continue to get the worst of both worlds: sporadic dispersal and congealed cities. Of course, in urgent compassion, symptoms must sometimes be treated: the urban poor, above all, cannot wait whilst structural changes take effect. But if such treatment, whatever form its subsidies take, is not part of some larger packet of countervailing remedies, it will compound the urban sickness by increasing the profit from land. It will feed the fever, just as surely as did the Expensive Site Subsidy which produced our post-war high-rise purgatory; it will set the poor in competition against the poor.

The constructive approach lies rather, in a recognition that, whereas formerly we thought of rebuilding our cities as a residual act in the wake of dispersal, now we have to recognize that any viable restructuring of our cities, as the primary aim, must also entail more dispersal from them. The chickens are coming home to roost, however, for those who were prepared to condone new towns only as public housing expenditure. Hence, since public expenditure must obviously be curbed, yet since the unit cost of provision in old cities is so much higher than elsewhere (it costs nearly twice as much to house a family in London, and at lower standards, as it does in the country at large), these people are now powerless to act. However, we are also told that what the country lacks is private investment. In so far, therefore, as the ground swell of dispersal may persist regardless of the state of 'growth', let new towns constitute such investment! In all of post-war experience, indeed, a more dynamic investment could scarcely be found. The new towns have engendered far, far more than their share of such vitality, of new forms of life, as Britain can own to. There, if anywhere, Britain is humming. Nor is the vein of imagination yet worked out; new styles of new towns—self-help, do-it-yourself, towns—are asking to be realized. It should be the purpose of public policy, then, to facilitate more such investments. And, ironically for all concerned, the Community Land Act is the instrument to hand.

All this, however, adds up to something less than a statement of faith. To find this, as so often, we have to retrace our steps. The key is to be found, I think, in the garden city idea, rather than the new towns. (The history of the transition from one to the other is of great interest for the history of ideas.) I am dealing now with nothing less than the question of the relation between the social and the physical worlds. Post-war planning, and not planning alone, has been beset by the irreconcilability of these different views of the world. The appearance of things and the social reality behind it— consider, if as an extreme, the case of Bath, with its tenements and offices behind a facade of eighteenth century living!— have constituted different language games: there are no conversion factors, so to speak, between them, no interpretations. And, in the vacuum between them, policy makes perpetual mischief and its makers cannot be called to account.

I submit that this situation only illustrates our distracted understanding of the world. The very idea we have of knowledge, as about an external reality only waiting to be discovered and appropriately labelled, underlies this schism between the physical and the social. Thus, as we remorselessly exploit the world on this basis of knowledge, we meet with these contradictions of values in our lives, more and more acutely. What the garden city idea did in these circumstances, instinctively and with much force, was to offer a reconciliation of these separate language games, based on a new form of life. We must, then, recover that intuition, so that no irreconcilability in our physical and social worlds shall arise. We could do it, I think, on an idea about cities that takes more from Howard's vision than from most current practice.

This is to project for planning a critical place in the contemporary reconsideration of ideas. It is, in fact, in the very nature of planning that it belongs there; environmental thinking, after all, is bound to challenge our presumptions about cause and effect. To do Marxism justice, it would claim the same central importance for urban forms in its own recasting of the human mind. The ideal communist city is one in which no persons live, only the masses. You can see the results, for instance, at Evry new town, south of Paris. The alternative—as also to the reproletarianization of our cities—lies with ourselves, in so far as we may recognize the part planning has to play in the present upheaval of ideas.

Of course, all this thinking seems to lead to the question, what is growth? I contend, however, the very question is false, and to answer it would be to accept the terms in which it is couched. At least, I would reject the simplistic notion (now being broadcast) that planning, when there is no growth, is about distribution. I think that would lead planners down desolate ideological roads. I would say, rather, that planning is about creating things: about the beneficent creation of urban forms, common to us all. There are lifetime's, and generations of lifetime's work ahead for planning thus conceived, regardless of what the state of 'growth' may be.

# INNER CITY LANGUAGE

Whatever their causes might be, and however complex, it is in our cities that the riots have been occurring. Cities, as cities, are the concern of planning. Yet the voice of planning, if not quite silent, has scarcely been heard in the resulting hubbub. Nor is this because planners themselves were taken by surprise by what has happened. Liverpool 8, for instance, has for years been a by-word in planning circles for the incipient violence of our cities. Moreover, ever since both the present and the last Government cut off the only escape route of the city poor, to the new towns, planners have well known the score. This deafness, rather, must be because the world has preferred to speak altogether a different language from planning.

Now, the normal language of our world—as we've made it for ourselves to live in—is quantitative. If things can be reduced to their parts, and counted, that makes sense to us. That is why money talks, as also why such stupifying efforts have been made with cost-benefit analysis to count whatever resists measurement. This is the world of materialism, of consumerism, of GNP and of our infinite expectations of what Nature will yield when we take her to bits and use these up. We all know what, say, 'wealth' means in that language, whilst the economists do not baulk at including the outlay on car accidents in GNP, and even the happiness of the greatest number has been counted.

Our cities, then, with the chance exception of certain major parks—ghostly reminders, as these are, of another world of values altogether—have developed as merely the residues of this language of quantities. They are full of business, and this business carries everyone along—so long as it operates: but if it stops—or, even more so, if you yourself suspend credibility for a moment and look with the eye of innocence at the concrete jungle for what it means, or at the detritus of any squalid city street—you will see an environment that simply cannot be accounted for at all in terms of the nobility of mankind.

This is why it is so significant that it is now ever more commonly said, money is after all not the answer. Whether or not this is because there is no money is beside the point. There is no money, it could rather be argued, just because it is not the answer: because we have thrown money until there is none left at problems like the inner cities (and at education and industry and housing, etc.), whilst, all along, the answers actually lay in the unquantifiable. But what else have we to live by? What other language do we know?

People have yet to realise that planning exists in terms of that other language, deriving its very rationale from it. This is, in fact, why planning has been the poor relation in our society, tolerated but ignored: why, even in its heyday, governments allowed it a few new towns, but deemed that, for the country at large, suburban sprawl and high-rise housing provided adequate environments. Planning, in other words, for all its impoverishments (many of which it has brought upon itself by abjectly mimicing its elders and betters) is embedded in the language of quality. As such, it holds riches that the politicians are vainly seeking elsewhere.

Planning, I would say, is about the creation of contexts—shall we say, environments?—within which meanings can be found in our lives. Meanings lie in the patterns in terms of which they make sense, and a pattern must conform to some totality if it is not to dissolve into chaos. That is why planning is about forms of settlements—whether cities, villages, towns, or regions—as wholes. Planning is holistic, not reductionistic, in its method. And this implies the language of quality, not quantity: the language of shapes and patterns and meanings and forms. In this language, 'wealth' has to do with the richness of our relationships and the warmth of communities. 'The only wealth', said Ruskin, 'is life', and I take it he meant the fullness that is possible only within the forms of our relationships.

In this light, the true bankruptcy of our cities consists in their meaninglessness. They have been centres of specialization, of professionalism, of competition between isolates, of 'excellence' for its own sake, of novelty for the sake of novelty—and of alienation, of anomie. Made as they were by isolated individual acts, they could hardly have been much more than the sum of their parts. How little gravity they exercise in themselves, indeed, is now being demonstrated by the Census; for the parts of which they have been aggregated are moving, to suit their separate conveniences, elsewhere. And when the pattern is gone from our lives, when our existence becomes meaningless, it is a common experience that human beings become violent. Violence, as fascism has always shown, is a kind of meaning. Or, putting it cynically the other way, if one is going to be unemployed, one might as well be unemployed in an agreeable environment—if one can get there. But there are many who can't.

That London, above all, has become meaningless—a kind of chaos—is demonstrated by the impotence into which the Greater London Council has fallen. The GLC had no other reason for its existence than to make sense of London and, ever since the debacle of the Greater London Development Plan, the Council has had no *raison d'etre*. That Plan was doomed because it tried (by the Herculean artifact of the Motorway Box) to make sense of London as it was. This would have left the structure of the city unchanged: that is,

monocentric, but abuzz with motorised traffic in a disem-
bodied atmosphere of frenetic activity. With the collapse of
that notion, the GLC abdicated from its responsibilities. Life
in the Brixtons of London has consequently become
disengaged from any totality in terms of which it might make
sense—except for expeditions of Paki-bashing to the
Southalls of London. In London, as elsewhere, the short-
comings of materialism, of the growth economy, the running-
down of the Cartesian knowledge machine, has simply
exposed the essential meaninglessness of life in the kind of
cities we have allowed to grow.

If planning, then, has lost touch, and even betrayed
itself, it is because it has forsaken its own ground. It has
allowed itself to be embraced by the Establishment—that
knowledge-ridden embodiment of power, centred in the
State—and has settled for a quiet life in the lower ranks of the
hierarchy. Planning has accepted that form follows function,
allowing the closure of village schools at the cost of the
village, or for urban motorways at the cost of the city. It has
abandoned its intuition, which should have told it that our
cities are simply impossible.

But why did it not say this, years and years ago? Well,
actually it did, and there were those on the old London
County Council and in Manchester and elsewhere who
listened and concurred. Had they not done so, there would
have been no new, or overspill, towns. But, since then, power
has seduced the old scheme of things. How else, indeed, can
one account for the inhumanity of the high-rise housing
movement except in terms of paranoia? In face of this,
planning's voice was puny in the extreme. And this power-
drive by the cities was inevitable, because their status was
intrinsically dependent upon the Centre, whose agents they
have increasingly revealed they are.

The cities, in the exploitation of their tenants and their
tenants' votes, have been riding the tiger of the State—and
now that tiger is consuming them. The problem of the inner

cities is therefore no less than an aspect of the constitutional problem of this country: of the concentration of power at the centre. Hence, in all these circumstances, the intuitive response planning has to make is to tell the unpalatable truth to the cities: you must lose the kind of power you have! (They have lost it, anyway, to the Government. The question is, what should be put in its stead?) The only viable power the cities can keep is, in fact, the power to preside over their own transformation.

Exhortations to rescue our society by a change of heart are notoriously futile. In this case, they are not necessary. All the signs are that the change is happening out of sheer disillusionment with the old order. To learn the holistic language of planning, then, would be quickly to turn the world upside-down—as it was last turned in the seventeenth century. It would mean, say, education that fitted the community, not what the pedagogs ordained. It would signify work that had meaning in an environment to which it did no violence. It would mean living with Nature, not using it. It would mean art that related to place—but was none the less sublime for that. It would mean, in other words, the very transformation of values that many are calling for. Of all this, however, the pre-requisite is that planning should reform itself and find its touch again. To do this, all it needs, fundamentally, is to recover its confidence.

Planning could recover its confidence by again talking its own language, and insisting that it be heard. This language would tell the world that there are no push-button solutions, that there is no short-term when it comes to the cities. The answers do not lie, mechanistically and deterministically, in what we do to the urban fabric, but in the meanings that fabric might lend us through the ways it is used: be they for schools from which truancy is merely the rule, or, conversely, say, for health-centres where the arrogant writ of medicine does not run. The business of planning is to put experts in their place.

In the cities we are involved in a tragedy which must be played out. the cities present the most daunting of challenges in the transition to a post-industrial age; in nothing else is there so much to be undone. Planning's first duty is to say, loud and clear, that our values have brought this on ourselves. Yet it is for planning also to say how the cities might be made meaningful again: be compartmented, perhaps, such that there is no city to be 'inner' to, and their village-like communities restored by giving precedence once more to form over function. If it said this, planning would become unpopular with its political masters, but it would be heard.

## GREEN BELT—OR THE GREEN CITY ?

More than any other single factor, it is to the hold of the green belt on the imagination that we owe the acceptance of planning in Britain. Like the planning system at large, the green belt cannot be given a monetary value and its benefits somehow 'proved'. It works, rather, by a process of dialogue and, ultimately, of human judgement. This process finds its rationale—such as it indeed must have—in the ideas we share about the forms our towns and cities should take. The green belt has been the great definer of those forms.

Yet how much longer can we rely on this talisman? Deep though its hold is—lying, no doubt, in the historical chambers of our minds, in the places where our civilization was nurtured—the present, in all its urgency, is knocking against the citadel of the idea of the green belt.

One symptom of this is the Government's demand that planning authorities should find 2,000 acres from London's statutory green belt for housing purposes. The Government simultaneously denies any threat to the green belt principle. Yet, of its nature, this is a principle that admits of no exception in practice. The green belt, if you like, is an illusion that depends on our unanimous acceptance of it. Only the deepest cynicism can ensue from any expedient abuse of it.

Indeed, to be fair, the Government's expediency is only

the tip of an iceberg of questioning of the principle of the green belt. It is our very life-style—so different from that which even recently was itself historically apt—that is asking if it is any more right or sufficient just to contain a city. This asking is forcing us to look again, in particular, at Abercrombie's appropriation of Howard's green belt idea, and question whether its transposition to the situation of London or Birmingham can still stand upon its own logic.

Retrospectively, one can well appreciate the yearning to restore form to the urban emptiness that suburban spread had made, by putting a ring around its further growth. But a belt, one supposes, has two edges. For Howard's *tabula rasa*—his schematic presentation of the social city—the page supplied the outer edge. For Abercrombie, the outer edge of the London green belt had no such comparable constraints in social geography. Indeed, as pressure on the inner edge has increased, with occasional nigglings into it, Governments have grandiosely expanded the outer edge, thus (they think) like knights in shining armour preserving the sacred principle of the green belt itself.

But, in fact, all such changes only bring under closer scrutiny the rationale of what Abercrombie stipulated. Where should it end, this process? It would be very surprising if the Government were not beginning to ask this question. For, on the one hand, they will already be as conscious as anybody that the green belt has been perverted into an instrument of social privilege, to keep green and pleasant what only the better-off can afford. And, on the other, they cannot be much longer over putting two and two together: in questioning, that is, whether the process of gentrification in parts of inner London, with its attendant stresses that are changing the social map of London, is not connected with the excessive premium the statutorily expanded green belt has put upon the mobility even of the better-off.

A green belt with virtually no outer limit is obviously a pernicious bottling up of the city, and there must come a moment when this brings the very concept under question. When this happens, however, there should be a pause for much deeper reflection. Merely to start gobbling instead of nibbling the green belt for housing would indeed be regressive. The lesson to be learned, rather, is that the green belt has played its part—its most destructive part—in keeping London the single-centred city it still is.

The green belt has formed just one of the rings of which the single-centred city is characteristically made. It has made the redeployment of that centre within the built fabric the more difficult; it increases the focus, from the city-region seen as a whole, of that centre. Consequently, its structural effect is to increase the stresses in the inner areas that derive from the values which such pressures create in the centre. Now, this is not to be read as a condemnation of the green belt as such. For many reasons, that must remain a valuable instrument of planning. Rather, it is to endorse the questioning of the logic of Abercrombie's application of the idea, and to say it must be adapted to a very different idea of urban structure than that to which historically we have been holding.

This new idea of urban structure, indeed, is one which lays no stress on any outer edge to the green belt—which, therefore, as much as discards the idea of a belt, as such. Yet, if this seems too much to ask, and even to put planning itself at risk (though, it should rather be said, planning is in danger from the weight of its own shibboleths) we have only to lift our eyes from our London preoccupation, towards the North.

The West Riding is in many ways a remarkable administrative county and its impending disappearance still cannot but call in question the whole basis of local government reform. In that county the green belt indeed statutorily exists, but to a pattern unrecognizable in terms of London's agonizing over the question. It exists, rather, as a green backcloth to a many-centred social city. If Yorkshire, then, can hold to this conception, why cannot we all? We should stop thinking about green belts, and start talking about the green city. The discussion cannot be much longer postponed.

# CHAPTER FIVE

# Rural Wholeness

# *Rural Wholeness*

## RURAL PLANNING

Planning can no longer take itself for granted. We no longer think that planning must be done as something too obvious to need justification. There are people who even seriously suggest there should be 'no go' planning areas from which planning should be debarred, and, whilst planning may still be generally accepted, there is widespread puzzlement as to its validity. Meanwhile, morale amongst planners themselves is disintegrating.

Before we face the question of planning for rural areas, therefore, let us try to understand what planning is in itself, what is its rationale? In my view this stems, both historically and logically, from the Garden Cities movement at the turn of the century. I do not mean by this that planning is about Garden Cities. I refer, rather, to the radical premise implicit in Ebenezer Howard's proposals: that we can make the places where we live. Our towns, cities and villages had hitherto been regarded as mere residues of other-minded actions. After 'Tomorrow: a path to peaceful reform' the possibility was there to be grasped, that our various forms of human settlement could be made and continuously re-made—not just received—and would be the better for it. Planning grew from that.

There is, of course, another strain to modern planning and one which even pre-dates the Garden Cities movement.

This is what I would call atomistic planning and it grew primarily out of the concern for public health and housing in the latter part of the nineteenth century. This strain is still with us and has been joined by others such as traffic engineering. But this sort of *ad hoc* bye-law planning does not, in my view, represent what we rightly think of as planning itself, if only for the reason that it makes no attempt to see things whole. And it is this attempt to see the forms of things, to see places as places, to set the stage, to see the wood for the trees, that is characteristic of what needs to be thought of as planning, and which distinguishes it.

This characteristic, however, has been both the strength and the bane of planning: the bane, because it has issued in the fallacy that planners are somehow omniscient. From this has duly stemmed the alienation that has come to be associated with planning: the we/them syndrome now so closely connected with it. This has happened largely because planners just have not known how to see the wood for the trees, but have tended to make a sum of all the trees and to call it a wood, mystifying both themselves and others in the process. Perhaps because our civilization is built upon the mode of atomization, of seeing the parts in order to understand the whole, of Cartesian reductionism, this has been the method to which planners themselves have weakly and anachronistically turned. (I have in mind that summation of all knowledge that goes under 'Corporate Planning'—and the situation has necessarily been compounded whenever academics have been called in aid.) The nadir of the business was probably the Inquiry into the Third London Airport, with its ridiculous dependence on cost-benefit analysis.

There are two complementary reasons for this state of affairs. The first was the repeal, in 1954, of the financial provisions of the basic planning legislation of 1947. This repeal was due as much as anything to the hanging of himself by the unfortunate Mr. Pilgrim, who had found he could not do

what he wanted with his own modest house except by paying
the public purse what he could not afford. (Mr. Pilgrim will
go down in the history, not only of bureacracy, but of
language itself, because the Act was impeccable in its
principles but also incomprehensible to such as Mr. Pilgrim.)
The Act had rationally enough allowed that the means for
making the places where we live should be provided by the
values generated by the communities who lived there, but it
was hopelessly unrealistic over the agencies of action.
Deprived of any means of action, then, planning ever since
has become merely reactive to developers: negative, not
positive, and therefore piecemeal.

The second cause of planning's failure to play its part, as
the one discipline concerned to see the wood for the trees, is
that planners became a profession, absorbed in technicalities
and no longer recognizing that planning's only rationale
consists in the development of the various forms of human
settlement—of towns, cities, villages, as such. Any recognition of this kind would perforce have had to be pursued
through that process of general dialogue out of which all our
perceptions of form are reached, and their language forged.
Instead, planners have allowed an illusion of themselves to
grow as being endowed with comprehensive knowledge,
whilst actually and necessarily cultivating an omniscient
secretiveness, out of which in fact only subjective decisions
could come. Planning has in practice rested upon (if
anything) a theory as to the hierarchy of settlements, and in
this hierarchy rural forms, by reason of smallness, have been
of a lower order of life and subordinate to urban forms. And
this has been sustained by ever more detailed analyses of
particular functions—shopping, industry, housing, education,
etc.—leading to the acceptance of policies that have done
much violence to the forms themselves of human settlement.
In such ways planning has achieved maximum interference
in affairs with minimum benefit.

Thus, most rural counties have operated planning

policies founded on the 'key settlement' principle, which would allocate certain functions to towns and villages, allowing some to survive and some to die—and some to neither live nor die. (Many a village, whilst denied all public investment, has survived by being transformed either into a commuters' dormitory or a geriatric ward. A countryside of class distincitons has thus been brought into being, with council housing only—and only council housing—in 'key settlements'.) But the greatest harm done by planning's failure to seize its historic role of seeing things in the large—and therefore differently from the way in which life is all too normally conducted—has lain in its incapacity to recognize any new forms of human settlement.

This has been most obvious in the case of the cities. The structure of cities has been changing radically under the influence of motorised mobility and increasing private affluence. The demands for space implicit in these changes are leading, by a simple enough logic, to cities that are many-centred, not single-centred as of old, and to a new form of settlement altogether, one commonly called the city-region. Planning's failures of perception in these respects have led to sheer loss of control of the urban flood, on the one hand, and on the other to such cruel and wasteful policies as high-rise housing, in an attempt to preserve the old form of single-centred cities, by manipulation of the needs of the poor. Underlying these failures, however, there has lain a still deeper tension. I refer to the distinction between our physical and our social ways of seeing the world and of putting it in order.

This difference has bedevilled planning with accentuated force as the old forms of urban life have vanished before our eyes. What does one do, after all, with a place like Venice or Bath: preserve the facades for a ghost population condemned to make tenements out of the fabric from which they have been the last to escape? Corbusier and his school conceived of the city in physical terms (to which a certain political ideology readily lent itself ) expressed by architectural monumentality for the masses. You can see a manifestation of this at Evry new town, south of Paris., which as it happens was located in a Communist commune. (It makes an interesting comparison with the bourgeois milieu of Cergy-Pontoise to the north.) By contrast, cities determined by social considerations in their crudest form—that is, the market—take on the amorphous character of the spread cities of America, deserts of suburban alienation. What weight then do we give to the physical and what to the social factors? Planners have not known the answer to this and in consequence the rationale of their practice has disintegrated still further.

Perhaps they can hardly be blamed for this. The relationship of Man to Nature is after all arguably the central problem of our times. In any case, whilst the conflict has raged on the social plane—as to whether the good city should be high rise or low rise—the counterbalancing campaign for the 'environment' has got under way and placed itself broadly in the path of urban development of any kind. In so doing it has gathered much support from those who want to keep the countryside just as it is, turning the formative concept of the Green Belt to their private advantage, so that they themselves can continue enjoying it to the exclusion of others, and for whom the relationship of Man to Nature is of much less interest than the cruder politics of ecology.

The fact is, indeed, that for planners themselves this question of how to measure the social against the physical is insoluble—so long as it is approached as if it might have some empirically verifiable solution. Actually, what we are dealing with here are two different language games—one about society, the other about the natural world. If any resolution of these two games is to be found I think it will lie not in the development of some new planning calculus but in common action towards some comprehensible goal. After all, it was the very potency of 'garden city' as an idea, that it combined the natural and the human in one artifact. I would argue that if planning is to recover its lost authority, this will need to be in terms of new forms of life, new patterns of human settlement, which once again will hold the prospect of resolving that tension between the natural and the social worlds which is so endemic to all our thought.

But it will not be easy to break the cast of mind that sees the country in its Picturesque and Romantic forms: particularly the village, which is still seen as a proto city, whose every vacant space should be infilled with housing before any more fields are built upon. I am sorry to tell you we have recently lost an Appeal at Dartington bearing upon this vital question. We had wanted to build two hamlets, each of about thirty-five houses, not within the village 'envelope', but just beyond yet related to its centre, in open ground which we wished simultaneously to dedicate to cultivation by those who would live in the two new clusters. This is 'part-time farming,' the opportunities for which are so deficient in this country. The concept was essentially ecological—of a balance between Man and Nature—but unorthodox in planning terms. In fact, however, although we lost the case, we won the argument, our Appeal being turned down on a technicality but the county planning authority (which had opposed us) being rebuked for interfering as it did. We therefore take heart and we shall not give up our effort to make new forms of rural life; nor shall we infill the village itself, but do our best to ensure that the open spaces within it are cultivated by those living around them. Thus we believe the breakthrough is near. I think that the relative shift of planning powers from the county, with its inevitably mandrinate attitude, to the districts is on balance to be welcomed and could prove fruitful of new forms of rural life.

In a sense, rural planning has had it too easy these past thirty years. With increasing farm size people have continued to leave the land, so planning has seen its job as rationalizing what was left: and to provide for fewer people, rather than for more, must always be easier. Supposing, however, the doctrines of scale and mono-culture in farming are at the end of the road: that the established social system and its wage economy contracts behind ever thicker defensive walls, leaving a perpetual and growing pool of 'structural unemployment' behind it—could the distribution of land for long be left out of the calculations of those of us who will want to know how the rest of society is to support life? (Particularly since, in present conditions, the investment needed to give agricultural employment to one man is of the order of £200,000 because of the capitalization now called for.) In these events, it is certain that planning will have to change its perceptions of the forms of rural life.

What I would plead, however, with all those who might understandably contend that events will outstrip any purpose that planning can serve, is not to throw the baby out with the bath water. What a shame it would be to commit, in reverse, the individualistic follies of the Industrial Revolution. The countryside still will need to be given form—new form. I do not think, however, these new communities will just happen—or not so happily as if they are given thought. I think, also, the new individualists of the countryside will find many surprising allies amongst the planning profession, which has absorbed many of the most caring young members of our society in recent years. I also suspect that the Development Commission, established nearly seventy years ago to restore life to rural areas, could prove an instrument of quite unexpected potency in the process of reasserting the values—the autonomous values—of rural life. (Even the machinery of State itself is not necessarily untouched by the spirit of the Age.) Perhaps the Development Commission will be persuaded that something is needed to replace the old, failed estates as dynamic centres of influence in the countryside: centres for the generation of a full life in the countryside. It might for example create agencies to implement positive development schemes in the countryside and to take risks if necessary—as local authorities are not able to do—in undertaking new enterprises. This goes beyond the simple supplying of funds; it provides the entrepreneurship as well and faces the risks. It does not have to interfere in any way with the present functions of bodies concerned with the countryside. This, at least, is what we have done at Dartington (which started as an attempt to re-create and to give new character and meaning to the form of the estate in order that it should truly serve its countryside.) English life is profoundly rural in its foundations; and we need to do something significant to rediscover our roots, and here perhaps the Commission can help—a colossal mission, as this dictates building up all the social, cultural and environmental components towards the full life that people should be able to live in a rural environment.

So I invite you to share my optimism about the times we live in. It is not based upon any return to an impossible past, but upon the conviction that we can create together the new forms of life in which Man and Nature might live harmoniously again.

# LEONARD ELMHIRST AND RURAL LIFE

At the last, and shortly before he left the shores of Britain to settle in America, all too soon to die there, Leonard Elmhirst's energies were concentrated upon the completion of a project very personal to himself. Those energies, in his late seventies, were still remarkable and, as I followed in the wake of his negotiations, I could only marvel at them. They needed to be remarkable, however, for he was forcing his will upon the ancient University of Oxford. He was resolved to bring about the amalgamation of two of its component bodies. One of these—the larger and more prestigious—was the Oxford Institute of Agricultural Economics, then headed by Colin Clark, an economist of international reputation: the other, the miniscule—in fact, the smallest component of the whole University—Oxford Institute of Agrarian Affairs.

Note the difference in their titles! The one was concentrated upon a narrow field of knowledge, yet carried much intellectual weight. The other covered a wide field, yet had but small acceptance. It was with the latter that Leonard's concern lay. He had founded it and sustained it, and had somehow prevailed upon the University to incorporate it. Of late, however, his Institute, constrained by its small resources, had become little more than the Secretariat for the International Conference of Agricultural Economists, which Leonard himself had been instrumental in founding, back in the 'Thirties.'

As such, the Oxford Institute of Agrarian Affaris still fulfilled an invaluable role—organizing those world-wide Conferences, and publishing their proceedings. The International Conference, indeed, from the start took an 'agrarian' view of its field: its economists had muddy boots, knew what it meant to farm, and recognized that farming was meaningless outside an agrarian context. Yet, by the time in question, that was already a losing battle. Economics, pure and simple, was by then rampant in the academic field. The fashion was for econometrics, and agricultural economics followed in its train. I can vouch that Leonard Elmhirst was saddened, if undefeated, by this scientific trend of thought.

He at least achieved his aim at Oxford. The two bodies were united, symbolically under one roof—Dartington House—provided by the Dartington Hall Trust. Leonard had successfully played the University at its own Byzantine game. And when, with Colin Clark's retirement shortly thereafter, Professor Ken Hunt of the Institute of Agrarian Affairs was appointed head of the joint Institutes, Leonard's scheme of things seemed fulfilled.

Yet—Professor Hunt's untimely death, shortly thereafter, aside—I think Leonard knew he had won a Phyric victory. He knew, I think, that without amalgamation the Institute of Agrarian Affairs could not have survived, and I think he must also have known its very approach to knowledge was doomed within the University. I suspect he was driven as much by a sense of responsibility towards those he had involved in his dream, as by any sense of completing his mission. Before he left Britain's shores, and the shores of life, he just wanted to leave things in order.

In thus closing his own book, Leonard Elmhirst left unexplained the springs of his beliefs. You must remember, after all, he stemmed from the West, and perhaps when he was perplexed it was only natural he should turn to Western values: to the supposed 'realism' of material things. Yet I think he only ever did so reluctantly and when he felt quite alone—and he must often have felt alone, surrounded by professionals as he was. For, in himself, it was not rationalism that animated him, but intuition: his feelings. And his intuition opened him to the wholeness of things: to the forms of life. I think his experience in the East sustained him in this approach through all the creative travails of his work, and singled him out for the remarkable person he was amongst us.

Yet, of course, like us all he was often perplexed, and so in practice he was a rich mixture of East and West. In the West, our idea of knowledge is to take things to bits to see how they work, and then we try to find some order in them. With one part of him, Leonard Elmhirst subscribed to this view. He was, for instance, a pioneer of artificial insemination in Britain, as of soil analysis, and he applied technology to the land in every possible way. He knew, however—as many others did not know—that in so doing he was tearing apart the fabric of rural life. Those others, I suppose, still put their trust in Providence, as their ancestors had done, to hold together what they had taken to bits. Providence, as we are now rather more aware, has somehow failed the West. I suspect, none the less, Leonard also had some trust in it—otherwise he would not have been the child of his times, the squire of Dartington, that he was—but he was also the possessor of two kinds of knowledgte, not one. He knew inwardly, as well as outwardly.

Inward knowledge, I mean to say, comes from practice, from learning by doing, rather than by reflective thinking. (One of Leonard's characteristic expressions was: 'It has to be lived'.) Being thus acquired, such knowledge is distinct from that dualism of observer and observed which typifies Western thought, best exemplified in its classical science. Hence, knowledge acquired by doing—by getting your boots dirty, or even by emptying the latrines, as Leonard shocked his Indian friends by doing—is not conductive to idealism, or Utopianism, for these constructs also oppose body to mind, appearance to reality. Leonard Elmhirst, rather, was a pragmatist, par excellence. In this, he took his cue from Thomas Jefferson, that great American champion of rural values, who, with Rabindranath Tagore, was the other main inspiration of Leonard's life. For Jefferson, America itself was an experiment, and that is how Leonard thought of Dartington: as the Dartington Experiment.

That explains, I think, why the Elmhirsts never built— or even considered building—a model village at Dartington, as several hundreds of well-meaning English gentry had done in the eighteenth and nineteenth centuries: 'well-meaning' is so far as those villages were the outcome of the enclosures of common lands for private profit. Nor was Leonard very interested in villages, as such. (They were, after all, only a development of the Late Middle Ages.) He was for many years (sixteen, I think) a member of the Development Commission: a Government Department set up at the beginning of the century to cope with the problems of rural depopulation. The Development Commission did much good work. Out of it, for instance, grew the Forestry Commission, Fisheries Research, the Rural Industries Bureau (now CoSIRA, the Council for Small Industries in Rural Areas), etc. But the Commission never looked at the forms of rural life— that is, at villages, hamlets, small towns—as such: as, for instance, planners must do. It looked only at their particulars, just as, indeed, Local Government in Britain looks only at services—like education, housing, roads, etc.

As a result, we have learned to our cost that those rural forms have become merely the functions of their services. Communities have been replaced by 'catchment areas'—so that when, for instance, some village school is closed in order to rationalize an education service, the village dies. Then, of course, we begin to worry—or rather, truth to tell, we are only now beginning to worry, because ironically today the English countryside is repopulating again, as the cities drain away!

So, if it seems strange that Leonard Elmhirst was not concerned with this, if villages did not seem to matter to him—if, indeed, 'community' was almost a dirty word with him—well, you have to remember that, just as Jefferson had America as his world, so Leonard had his estate at Dartington, and this was world enough.

Dartington, I think one might say, was Leonard Elmhirst's ashram. It was the whole of life, where head and heart and hand were to hold equal sway. And wholeness was, I think, intrinsic to Leonard's practice of learning by doing, and to his intuitiveness. That is why he at least recognized that technology of itself could tear the fabric of rural life asunder, and why its introduction must be accompanied by measures to repair that harm. For, of course, he believed in rural values. And rural values, I submit, have to do with ways of life as a whole, and hence with what is qualitative rather than quantitative, and with the meaning of belonging; in contrast to urban values, which have to do with quantities, with the fragments that are reducible to what is measurable, with things rather than process and with 'doing your own thing'—and between these two is a gulf which cannot be bridged, despite what sociologists would like us to believe, by suburban life, or even any of the contemporary miracles of communications' technology.

For Leonard Elmhirst, however, this wholeness of life consisted just in balancing one specialism with another . . . and with another, in all their profusion—as in some project like the Tennessee Valley Authority. So, if you say that this balancing must in the end beg the question of the context in which it all makes sense, I would agree. But I would say in Leonard's defence that the forms of rural life had ceased to exist (and still do not exist) in which a full life could truly be lived. The village, that is to say, by this century—and certainly after the trauma of the Great War, which I think destroyed the spirit of rural England—had ceased to provide a vessel adequate to contain people's aspirations—perhaps, above all, because the Church at the heart of it had lost its conviction: the congregation had become better informed than the priest, and in 1916 Leonard himself abandoned the idea of entering the Ministry. The countryside, I would therefore argue, must now evolve new forms to give meaning to the possibilities of modern technology—for without form there is no meaning, and without meaning all our inventiveness, all our knowledge, even, and the material wealth it brings, is hollow.

Leonard Elmhirst was a pioneer of that search, and his integrity was too great for him ever to proclaim he had accomplished it—at Dartington, or anywhere else. He was wise enough to know you do not attain rural values simply by building a village, and perhaps that is true anywhere in the world. But I can tell you, as one who followed him at Dartington, that search is at least an antidote to rural stagnation. Leonard Elmhirst's Dartington is still in process.

# AN ALL TOO HUMAN PLACE ?

You can't read Dartington on the ground. The road signs say 'Please drive carefully through the village', but you'd be hard put to identify the 'village' amongst what seems like a haphazard scatter of buildings around you. Physically, the place is really a parish of hamlets, some old, some new, and the Hall itself is out of sight, up the hill a mile away. If you'd heard of Dartington before, and perhaps thought you were going to see some up-to-date, Bauhaus version of the picturesque villages of the eighteenth and nineteenth centuries, yet giving form to a new idea of rural life, you'd be at a loss. Nonetheless 'Dartington' assuredly exists, more vitally than any petrified National Trust village, and I want to write here about how it may be understood.

The Elmhirsts, who founded Dartington—he, Leonard, the impecunious son of a small Yorkshire estate owner; she, Dorothy, an American of the Whitney family and of a disposition as radical as she was wealthy—defined their purposes little more than by saying they wanted to show that a rural life could be as full as any urban one. To do this, they wished to use and revive an old and decayed estate, because the English estate has historically been the centre of our rural civilization, servicing and influencing (whether you judge for good or ill) the countryside around it and in manifold ways. What they set out to do, in effect, was to give a new meaning to the estate as a form, and this is why Dartington and its activities are now generically referred to by those living there as 'the Estate'—although this is, indeed, by now unrecognizable in terms of what generally happens on estates, whether rural or urban.

The vagueness of purpose was, I think, not unintentional. Utopia was always eschewed at Dartington: there is no belief there in a predetermined state of perfection. It's true that in the early days the notion of 'community' was in frequent use—but not for long. 'Community' had come to be associated, in those days (the mid-twenties), with dubious projects, which looked to some rather precious harmony between people of common purpose, such as experiences like Robert Owen's New Harmony, alas! showed never to have existed. (I think, however, this debasement of the word is now ended, and it has a new coinage.) Dorothy, I think, sought to the end of her life for the unity in our distracted world that would make sense of it; yet hers was an essentially private search. As for Leonard, to the end of his days (and he died at eighty) he resisted any attempt to specify the essence of Dartington. I remember him showing a rare temper when once such an attempt was being made. There had been a day-long discussion concerning overall policies amongst a score of management people at Dartington, to which Leonard contributed but little, when towards the end, and perhaps sensing that he as the ultimate point of reference would not be there much longer, an attempt was made to elicit from him what 'Dartington' actually was. Leonard's hot-tempered reaction was that he would have no part in the establishment of any 'Benedictine rules'.

In fact, however, I think it can be said that Dartington is a religious place, and in this respect it has been a precursor of one significant aspect of today's Alternative movement. I mean by this that Dartington has always been mindful of the spirit that animates an otherwise mechanical universe. The 'full life' is after all not plausible without this consideration.

But I think Leonard and Dorothy would both have agreed with Wittgenstein, that there has been too much spoken of that of which one must be silent. Many observers have felt, of course, that without some common faith an entity so complex as Dartington, and with such a diversity of people and activities, could not hold together. The great potter Bernard Leach, for instance, who worked at Dartington in the 'thirties and has remained close to it since, speaking from his own faith as a Bahai, is on record as saying that this lack of a 'church' for Dartington would prove its downfall. Yet I suspect Leonard was right in thinking that the opposite would be the case: that if ever it became a church, its downfall would be assured.

What, then, holds the thing together: farms and forestry with music, education with textiles, glass-making with theatre, research with furniture manufacture, crafts with computers, retailing with art, gardening with building? It is plausible to argue that this phenomenon can be explained by a combination of the security of the Trust's wealth, on the one hand, with people's normally repressed idealism on the other. There may be some truth in this, even if only because some people probably do become too comfortable at Dartington; they cease to be adventurous once under its shelter. The Trust has certainly been seen as a mini Welfare State, and with a bottomless purse at the service of all good causes. It also struggles continuously with the paternalism to which its structure makes it prone. Yet I very much doubt if any such charitable concept would attract, as Dartington continues to do, the adventurous spirits who almost embarrass us by their efforts to work here whenever the opportunity offers, and in no matter what branch of our affairs. And, anyway, the Trust is no longer wealthy, if it ever was; inflation has seen to that, such that our survival now depends overwhelmingly upon our own efforts, rather than upon inherited wealth. More- over, I would claim that actually the Trust's wealth has always been put to work in adventurous ways, such as do not

ultimately consort with any merely cynical view of Dartington's existence. Many who have been given the opportunity
to sink or swim, indeed, have sunk.

I think, rather, that the explanation for the continuing
attraction of Dartington is to be found in very much the same
region as that which supplies the aspirations of an Alternative
Society. And I do not think this source has much to do with
frustrated idealism. That frustration has been with us I would
argue, since Plato. On the contrary, I would say that the deep
surge of change we are witnessing today is to do with a
profound rejection of idealism and all its fruits. It is about
nothing less than replacing whatever it is that has given
European civilization its spurious mastery of the world,
because people are becoming more and more concerned with
the consequences. You must excuse me if I only say (in
shorthand) that I think what is being rejected is idealistic
thought itself—and excuse me, not least, because this will no
doubt seem shocking. I must simply leave it, that this shock is
some measure of the change in the midst of which we live.

At all events, I think Dartington remains of interest to
those who gladly accept the diversity and even the contradictions of life—the many points of origin that even rational
actions can have—not its illusionary uniformity: who seek
the questions, not the answers. And this language of
uncertainty, I think, is the language of the future. We shall
surely learn to live with it—and we will be enabled to do so
because it is to the strengths of human personality itself that
increasingly we shall be looking. In this respect also, then,
Dartington is in tune with the 'alternative' world. If
Dartington were just an exercise in rural regeneration it
would already be dead: a mere model for endless repetition by
a moribund bureaucracy—the sort of thing, say, that doomed
India's post-Independence village movement, once inspired
by Gandhi and Tagore. (Leonard Elmhirst had acutally been
Tagore's secretary, and had established the rural institute of
Tagore's ashram/university at Santiniketan.) It is not,

however, just a vagueness in the objectives of Dartington that allows scope for this cultivation of diversity, but a certain very positive concern: one for the person as a person. For this reason, then, one can actually say that what has saved Dartington (though there are those who would not like to hear it) has been its School.

Not surprisingly, the School has also become the most divorced part of the Estate. (One could be forgiven for thinking sometimes that its spiritual home was, say Hampstead, not Dartington at all.) This, however, is how it has had to survive economically in a world, to which Dartington after all belongs, in which people are conventionally seen simply as actors of roles, as parts of the social mechanism—no matter how liberal a society it may be—and for which education is perceived as the conditioning process. Consequently, the School has had to go where it could to find parents and children who do not view education just as an investment, or in social engineering terms, and who are prepared to face the risk (casting their bread upon the waters) of a child being just itself. As a result, at least, the School has never lapsed, like so many other 'progressive' schools, into mere liberal institutionalism. It's still for real, in classical 'progressive' education terms: an on-going revolution, simply because the child as a person is always unpredictable and can take you anywhere. If there is ever an alternative politics, then, this will surely condition its education programme.

It could be argued that the School at Dartington is itself out of touch with 'reality'. This may be so, but not because as a fee-paying school it is founded on a class structure that seems no longer tenable: 'class' is precisely not recognizable as a reality to an education of, and for, the person. (Is this why the School generates such hostility among the educational Establishment?) Rather, if the School is out of touch, it is quite conversely, because its curriculum is not yet emancipated from the academic notion of knowledge about reality that 'subjects' supposedly reflect. The original notion of the working Estate as the very classroom of the School simply proved premature. We may yet get back to it. In the event, the School has never been completely persuaded of the idea of 'pure knowledge', which bedevills English education, but rather, through the agency of the child as performer, still espouses such knowledge as has its place in life. The point is, that without the School surviving in its romantic ghetto of the spirit these last fifty years, Dartington itself could have become just another arid blue-print of the social engineers. As it is, it is not just a machine to be replicated.

I mention these internal factors only to illustrate the difficulties of pigeon-holing Dartington. (As Leonard used to say—it was his whole educational philosophy—to 'understand' something, it has to be lived!) Perhaps the first reflective step towards understanding Dartington then, is to recognize that it is founded upon a qualitative nexus; and, since the world we have made and which we inhabit is founded upon the reduction of all this to a quantitative nexus, these difficulties of understanding can well be imagined. They call, in fact, for a different kind of understanding altogether. Essentially, this treats of all forms of life, each in its own right, and without seeking to reduce them to some common denominator (which in practice can only mean money). The general qualities with which Dartington is concerned, then, are nothing less than those of a rural life; and this raises the crucial question as to whether such values obtain any more, or whether in fact the differences between urban and rural are not diminishing and should be allowed to disappear?

If this meant that to preserve the quality of rural life it must revert to being nasty, brutish and short. I would of course agree to the merger in question. If, however, it meant that rural life could only become a sort of second-grade urban life—with 'Opera for all' with a piano, instead of an orchestra—I should demur. The countryside is indeed in some danger of this kind of urbanization, with the closure of village schools upon essentially urban assumptions as to size and the rationalization of 'knowledge,' and of cottage hospitals likewise. Yet I don't think these are the only, or even the real, options. I think, rather, there will abide a meaning of that which is 'rural' in quality, and that this meaning will strengthen and grow.

I say this because I think that rural qualities are tied to things that are personal in life—in contrast to the essential impersonality and alienation of urban life—and that things on the personal scale—for which we use what Martin Buber called the 'I-Thou' word, in contrast to 'I—It'—are what are increasingly thirsted for. And just as we are told that our robins in Britain are tame because we treat them in that way, whereas in many parts of Europe, though living in the hedgerows, they are never seen by Man, so I like to think at Dartington this rural quality is nourished. This is not to denigrate urban life, which of course has its enduring qualities also. What has to be accepted, rather, is that qualitative differences cannot be reduced to quantities: which means, say, that urban and rural poverty are quite different things and cannot be reduced to monetary terms—though neither are to be tolerated for that reason.

If, then, there is this solid base for Dartington in the continuing validity of rural life, of what forms does it consist? Well, we are coming close to the way in which I think it can be understood; and this way of understanding is as important as the thing in itself: is, in fact, the thing itself. There are several forms of life at Dartington: industry, the arts, education, agriculture, commerce. Each has its language, and if Dartington were the world at large, that would be that. But at Dartington we strive, not so much to understand one another's language, as not to misunderstand it. (What is more divisive than the common words of different language games?) This does not mean that each person is a dabbler in various specialist areas. It means, rather, that some at least of the perennial criteria of human action are in the common currency of speech, the grammar, of Dartington. Money is, of course, one such currency and, though it is but one of these, it is none the less important. But this means that a question such as what are 'profits?' is of legitimate concern to anyone, not just to those in business. For if no ethical criterion is absolute, then each may be qualified wherever its writ runs. And anyway, might not the arts or education, say, even be asked to become more 'profitable'?

Land is another such archetypal criterion that is of particular concern to Dartington. Land, too, has its own reasons that Reason knows not of. (That, after all, is why land-use planning exists. You don't make, or re-make, a town just by market forces; if you did, how would you value Hyde Park?) There are things that are right, or not right, as China has understood for thousands of years, about how land is used to make the countryside. Land is thus the legimate concern of everyone at Dartington. Likewise, there is the immemorial dialogue about people: about the person as a person—the question, I should say, from which Christianity started. As the Stoics had it (before Plato put them down): Man is the measure of all things. This dialogue, also, as I've already said, is endemic at Dartington. And then there is all that currency of speech to do with design: with the rightness of the things we make. This is no more the private province of the arts than money is of business—or should not be. And so on: it is to do with the re-making of the grammar of the forms of life.

There is nothing unusual in each of these pregnant areas of discourse. What is perhaps unique at Dartington is that they even tentatively relate, and that everyone is thus admitted to a whole family of meanings. This is our kind of 'democracy' of shared languages. What this betokens—and wherein I think the significance of Dartington lies—is that we are a-swim, immersed, in the human dimension, which is that of language. We are exceptional in this respect only because the West at large has long ignored its own human dimension by assuming that language is merely a mirror of ultimate reality, not a kind of reality itself, and, in striving to capture that reality, has but dehumanized itself by compartmentalizing life. Because of its modest scale, then, Dartington's sheer complexity allows it to be what it is: an all too human place, one exposed to all the rawness of being human.

Do not assume, please, that when I talk of language I am only thinking of words. There are, rather, many languages— not by any means least, that of action. It is the human condition itself I am concerned to draw attention to in so far as Dartington shows it. So if you pass through Dartington and cannot read the landscape, remember that appearances are not reliable guides to reality. Please allow that your very inability to read Dartington could suggest that it is a place too busy creating itself to have lapsed into the conventional trap of commemorating itself.

Lastly, it may well be the case that the language I have been using about language might not be comprehended by many at Dartington itself. The language of the Textile Mill, say, or the Joinery Works, or even the College of Arts, may be much more about pay and conditions of work than about excellence, or people, or place. The Social Club, likewise, has some seven hundred members whose main focus is on beer and skittles. Certainly, all these are forms of communication to be respected in their own right. Yet I think 'Dartington' exists—and there is much evidence for this—because it holds the possibility to which people aspire for a fuller, a more human, identity: the possibility of partaking in all such discourse as being human makes us freemen of. This is a freedom, to be sure, which accepts life's contradictions and all its variety, rather than either limiting everyone to their own 'business' or reducing everything to some ideology of the truth.

That we share so many languages, then, ought to provide for a rare generosity of spirit, because it should allow us to put our trust in the rules of the game of life itself. If, then, this generosity is sometimes missing from Dartington it is perhaps because, paradoxically but inevitably, we attract idealists ripe only for disillusionment. Beer and skittles remain our best defence against any such pretensions. But if there is nevertheless constant strain in the community of Dartington, as any other, rather than perpetual harmony, I think it is because the wholeness of it all makes calls upon what is human in us to the uttermost.Is this to say it should be abjured? Not, I submit, if our lives themselves are to have meaning.

# OF PLACE AND OF SPIRIT

Lewis Mumford has written of how it was, when the clocks first chimed the hours across the fields from the towers of mediaeval churches, that men's minds began to change. The churches were surely there before the clocks were placed in their belfries. Certainly, they were not established to convey a clockwork message—a message that neither minarets nor stupas carry. Yet nowadays, such is the change that indeed has occurred, although those churches are (if we are lucky) still part of the rural scenery, they are no longer implicit to the countryside's way of life. The scenery would be depleted, to be sure, were they to disappear, but even the older inhabitants would somehow manage without them, having so many different things to do, all regulated by the hours. The clocks Mumford spoke of were in fact tolling a knell for their hosts.

I don't know if there was any theological controversy over the churches' welcome to those clocks. That they were placed in the belfries, however, would have conformed to the primacy which, by the early seventeenth century, knowledge had been accorded in the West. That there might have been an underlying anguish is perhaps best suggested by Isaac Newton's long obsession with alchemy in his middle years, seeking a resolution of this new knowledge with his secret (Aryan) faith. In the result, anyway, ours is a knowledge-driven society. The reductionism by which this knowledge has proceeded has, by the proofs it offers, overpowered any doubts there may have been, at least in the Protestant world, about this road to Truth. But in so doing, I suspect it disintegrated the sense people had once made of the rural way of life, of which their churches had been an integral part.

My scholarship is alas! non-existent when it comes to stringing together such poignant rural English phenomena as, say, the Peasant Revolt, the roving beggar bands of Tudor times, the Diggers, Levellers and Quakers, the Enclosures and the Poor Law. I suppose the Marxists have got it all figured out. I only want to say that through all those historical resonances I seem to hear a question about personal identity: about where a person belongs, thereby confirming his or her existence—and about the loss of it. I suspect that where a person belonged, the community around him, was taken for granted—as God-given—before the Age of Knowledge. The taking of this away from him by the growth of knowledge has thus been akin to an increasing consciousness of Self, of one's nakedness.

By now, the fortune Dick Whittingtron sought on the streets of London is easier for us to appreciate than the state of affairs he left behind him in the countryside, which we discount. The cities, in fact, became the arenas of life for the technological games we have all since learned to play. And out of this there arose the distinction between urban and rural values.

Now it is fashionable in our times to say that the distinction between urban and rural values is disappearing. We all see the same television, read the same newspapers, are consumers of the same pap, all originating in the cities. Indeed, as Chairman of the Town and Country Planning Association's Executive Committee you might well remind me of Ebenezer Howard's famous diagram of the three magnets—that very logo of settlement planning: namely, the counter attractions of both Town and Country , and their resolution in Garden City. I certainly wouldn't want to question that analysis—at least, not the part of it concerned with how we would like to have our cake and eat it. But I think that today we find ourselves in the face of forces which suggest that much deeper currents are flowing, just as perhaps they have always done beneath the surface of events.

I am thinking, that is to say, of much more than the spreading suburbanism of this century. That, after all, is nothing new. London was already spreading beyond its disused city walls by the sixteenth century. On the less settled mainland of Europe, to be sure, city walls continued for centuries to serve a purpose—in Paris, up till 1870—but of late their city sprawl has been catching ours up, fast. The process, in fact, is merely the tail-end of something—namely, of the search for privacy, with the Common Man now taking for himself what his Lord had already acquired by the fourteenth century: he had by then a chamber of his own, apart from the common life of the Hall. Rather, I have in mind the growing expression of a need of which this very suburbanization makes only nonsense.

This observation, in fact, leads me to ask what really is the distinction between urban and rural values? To consider the Dick Wittingtons of our own day, what makes a Bengali peasant leave the land and take his chance in the living Hell of Calcutta? One knows the statistics about Indian rural poverty, the indebtedness and over population, and perhaps also about the claustrophobia of village life; but even so (or so it seems to me) there must be something very powerful at work to bring those masses to the inhuman squalor of Calcutta. Obviously (but is it the root of the matter?) in the Third World generally the same forces of materialism are now working upon men's minds as once so powerfully created cities in the West. It is thus strange—perhaps even tragic— that the Eastern respect for process should be succumbing to the potency of objects to be acquired just when its deeper validity is being recognized in the materialistic West.On this basis alone it would seem that urban values are concerned with the possession of things, and hence with what is quantititive, with what can be measured and against whose 'growth' we hope to measure ourselves: whereas rural values, I would say, are to do with ways of life, with wholes and what is qualitative, and hence with where we belong. Yet, because we are encaged by language (rather than rejoicing in its cadences), we do not realise, say, that urban 'poverty' and rural 'poverty' are different in kind. Indeed, our misapprehension about language—our assumption that it is but the mirror of some reality, and hence that statistics speak the truth—is at the root of our materialism and its manifold illusions. For what is this 'I', or 'We', so inseparable from, yet antipathetic to, materialism?

It is, indeed, this rising concern for identity in a world now depersonalized—a world in which things are venerated rather than persons, and in which human beings too are treated as objects—that to my mind gives its continuing importance to rural values. I know it could be said that in the East their aim has been to lose the self, whereas in the West ours has been to find it, and perhaps this helps make the Calcuttas of this world acceptable to some. I would only want to make the point that any civilization that gives primacy to knowledge in order to achieve mastery of the world will not recognize until it is too late that it has jeopardized the meaning of what it knows: that our lives must have a context, a place to be, and without which materialism can confer no identity.

Of course, the sub-culture of our civilization shows that this need has continuously been felt: it has supplied the counterweight to the dominant rationalism of the Age of Knowledge. Thus, the imagining of Utopias synchronized with the emergence of scientific enquiry, starting with Bacon's fragments of 'New Atlantis'. And more powerfully, Romanticism became the compensatory shadow of Industrialism (and not, surely, the converse!): the evocation of Natural Man, and hence the hero and the Artist, as the quintessential person, beyond society and the law, for even the industrial Establishment has realized that without the arts we would be inhabiting a desert. Progressive education—keeping alive the notion of the child as a child—has been another example of this neccessary subculture, flying in the face of conventional practice. Whilst out of Romanticism also came perhaps the first measures to create for 'ordinary' people places in which they could belong and make sense of their lives.

It may be ironical that the villages of the Picturesque movement were to a large extent a function of the Enclosures. Whatever the miseries on the negative side of that account, however—or perhaps because of them—the spiritual need to which the Picturesque movement responded is not to be decried. There are, in fact, hundreds of such villages in Britain, built in the eighteenth and nineteeth centuries at the manor gates, for the mutual comfort supposedly of the squire and his tenants. However, the most significant, as also poignant, endeavours to compensate for the vanishing context of everyday rural life was, to my mind, seen in the Shaker communities of North America.

The Shakers' attempt to reconcile technology (which of its nature divides us) with community was built upon a theology founded, significantly, in the feminine principle. The Shakers were, also, above all practical people, born of the Industrial Revolution, and were for generations leaders of invention in agriculture, whilst the marvellous restraint in the design of their artifacts was a standing testimony to the spirit which their technology sought to serve. Their very celibacy—psychological incubus though it must have been—was a breath-taking challenge to humanistic Utopianism (and perhaps a death-wish born of industrialism), for they accepted its logic of human extinction as the corollary of our each finding God. Not for them the Millenium, with its consolation of children for another thousand years! No wonder that they had the strength to last so long—even though materialism seduced them too in the end! Other urban villages, such as Bourneville and Port Sunlight, built by enlightened capitalists, together with Robert Owen's Utopian experiments, were further symptoms of the spirit that was then so evidently wanting to be nourished. It is amazing indeed, how bright a light these relatively puny ventures shed against the vast darkness of Victorian industrialism.

It was out of these beginings, that the modern concept of planning grew, with its genesis in the Garden City. It is saddening how soon one can only look back at the disintegration of a noble idea: at its institutionalized degeneration. The wholeness was lost, as it was bound to be once planning was universalized. Bureaucracy soon reduced it to manageable parts—manageable, that is, by central government. Consider, for instance, the notorious policy of Key Settlements that governed post-war rural planning. This policy conceived of settlements in terms of the provision of functions. By this submission to technology, then, rural planners have ensured that function and its 'catchment areas' should supersede community, rather than that a community should determine the kind of services appropriate to it. Or rather, they have ensured the cultural impoverishment of such communities as could survive their ministrations, reducing countless villages to cosy shells for commuters.

Of course, it would have been a bold planner who said that villages should have, say, the education appropriate to them, rather than that laid down by the remote County Education Committee, which in its turn only applied the conventional wisdom about education as knowledge divided into 'subjects,' and therefore taught in schools, regardless of their community, with catchment areas large enough to provide Sixth Forms of an 'economic' scale. Or who contended that hospitals do have a human dimension, which should override whatever catchment area the latest bit of medical technology may require to confer economic viability upon it. Or who said that rationalizing the latest technology of sewage disposal should not be allowed to debar the development of a village as a village. But it was out of just such boldness that planning was originally conceived, if it was about anything at all. That was the vital contribution it had to make—the seeing of the wood from the trees. Planning's failure, then, has left us all with places less and less worth belonging to, not least because of the social class divisions that Key Settlement policy, through its concentrations of public housing, has brought into our villages.

One consequence of that failure (or perhaps a cause of it) has been a poverty of ideas about new forms of rural life. Only the stereotypes of settlement form have been accepted for Key Settlement purposes—whether as the hosts of statutory services, or for abandonment by them—and 'infilling' has been the order of the day, turning villages into pro-cities and depriving them of open land for small scale food production. Only the emergent reality about the economics of agriculture is likely to break this cast of thought. For high plane agriculture has been one of the main technologies determining rural planning policy, and land around the 'envelope' of villages has been preserved for it.

But what is that 'agriculture' for which we are urged to preserve the land? It is something through which, by increasing unit scale of production and inputs of energy, successive governments have sought to ensure this country's self-sufficiency in food, in a world in which we indeed find ourselves precariously placed to pay our way. And yet, for years now, the resultant agri-business has brought us little nearer to that goal, of which we still fall far short—and shorter still, as the logic of Europe's Common Agricultral Policy works itself out. It is no longer any secret that British agriculture is at a loss to know which way to turn.

In these circumstances, I don't think we can avoid

developing some new kind of agriculture. Farming is over-capitalized and, however it is brought about, the redressing of that ratio will mean more people on the land again, using more appropriate machinery. And if this is to be so, the scale of the problem is such that the very pattern of the countryside must change.

I am speaking, ultimately, of a new symbiosis of man and the land, and if this implies changing the pattern of the countryside we have inherited from the Enclosures, there could be historic justice in that. There is a new rural landscape to be made, one that speaks of a different spirit from that which imbued the romantic picture of England we now so unquestioningly admire. The hamlets, or isolated holdings, which would form the nucleii of this new rural life would be the expression of quite as urgent a sense of purpose as any that have shaped our landscape in the past.

In mentioning such nucleii of a new rural society, however, I do not mean to speak mechanistically. Certainly the land will need to be cultivated by people both more numerous and closer to it if it is again to make its contribution to a more meaningful society, and this will be conducive to a settlement pattern in which the hamlet is bound to figure strongly. This will not happen only for 'economic' reasons. I think it will happen, rather, because people need to re-discover meaning in their lives, and many of them will seek this in places of a human scale in which they are engaged in activities of an intelligible immediacy. In other words, the very idea of what is 'economic' will change. Yet should the exterior and the interior resolutions of our needs coalesce it would be no coincidence. For both derive from the same source: from the hubris of our knowledge, which has culminated in depriving Man of both Nature and himself.

Beyond new hamlets, however, there is the question of new life-styles. The form of life our cities have generated is breaking down because the heart has gone out of it; these communities of disparate knowledge have turned into clouds of atoms, and are dispersing. But just to transplant that urban life-style to small towns and villages will solve little. I doubt if people's hunger for identity will for long be satisfied, say, by doing a job, conventionally speaking, in some small community that is only a microcosm of the city. It is the community, not the job, that must confer any satisfying identity. The concept of a 'job', in fact, is what itself is really under question, and is beginning to look increasingly like a short-lived abberation of the industrial age.

It would be surprising, moreover, if people in a post-industrial society were satisfied with the somewhat attenuated kind of community that even the best of our small towns and villages can offer today. Such communities, by their human scale, do indeed make possible the warmth of contacts with numerous acquaintances for which some of us have, of course, much reason to be grateful. But a more deeply satisfying community, surely, would be one in which, for instance, the Buddhist notion of 'right livelihood' (brought to our attention by Schumacher, and practised by the Briar-patch group in San Francisco) obtained: such that work, rather, took the place of the job, and in which people could partake of the work to be done. I speak, I realize, in terms of a paradigm shift. But—and far different from the discredited idealistic concept of the commune—I think such new kinds of communities are not inconceivable.

What I have in mind is something more akin to the historical model of an estate, or even of the monastery. Obviously, I do not mean to reproduce these, as such: that would be to mistake shadow for substance. Yet if it is the balance between person and world we are now forced to reconsider—to say nothing of the dualism that has brought us to that reconsideration—it is to those ancient forms we might helpfully return to extract the wisdom that lay in them.

Superficially, it was a common creed that held those forms together—and, of course, subordination to the authority of that creed. But, more profoundly, I think it was a common language: or rather, a common grammar. There were, after all, many skills, each with its language within, say, even a Benedictine monastery—for the monasteries were arguably the cradles of the industrial and agricultural revolutions. Yet each such skill was sacramental. They thus partook of one grammar; each one could be mediated to the other. All, in Isiah's terms, belonged to God's Holy Mountain. That Mountain, however, was actually the astounding totality of language. And such a mountain—or rather, range of mountains—could be found again: not creedal, but evoked by the same mystery—a mystery that words heaped upon words can never surmount. These mountains, then, would be communities that shared this mystery because they shared their diverse languages—and so recognized that no one language explains our existence here.

To be practical—and what I'm saying comes out of practice, at Dartington—I think that out of the ever more apparent illogicalities of our present world a new order of communities is bound to emerge. These would not be communities of common ownership. Nor would they be communities in which nobody had more skills, or other skills, than anybody else. They would not be egalitarian communities in which all the languages (and of course I do not mean tongues: but the manifold languages of knowledge) were open, not closed, discipline by discipline: communities in which the artist, say, was prepared to accommodate his art (and perhaps become a craftsman thereby), the entrepreneur his wealth (and perhaps modified his pursuits accordingly), the farmer his cultivations (and perhaps changed his practices thereby), the doctor his diagnoses (and perhaps treated the whole patient by seeing him in context of the community), and so with the carpenter, the merchant, etc.

There is conceivably a common point of reference of all these disciplines, other than that (the sacramental) which obtained in the past. It stems from a recognition that reality—

whatever it is—is not that which language describes. Such a recognition would imply that carpenter, merchant, doctor, farmer, entrepreneur and artist shared their knowledge, not just so far as others could understand it in its own terms, but by modifying those terms—and hence even that knowledge—so that they made sense in the context of the community as a whole.

I can, however, think of no foundation for communities of this kind other than submission of human beings to the rights of the natural world—in contrast, that is, to their present exploitation of it. Nor can I imagine how this change would come about by some conversion of mankind on the road to Damascus, but only by force of circumstances. Happily (yet misfortuately) this is precisely what is likely to happen to us as Nature, as always, has the last laugh. But I think we should prepare for it by creating now the nucleii of these quasi-monastic communities of the future. And it follows in all logic that, in such communities, knowledge would not be that which is derived from abstract thought, but that which is lived, and the living shared. I want further to suggest that there is an insatiable thirst in people to partake of what, in the last analysis, cannot be explained, but only lived.

In sum, the drive to find meaning in our lives has a spiritual force. Those restless tides of humanity—once of rural depopulation, now (in the West) of urban—are in search of a pattern for their lives: in search at least as much, so to speak, of their daily grammar as of their daily bread—though they may have thought they saw the pattern in the bread. Either way, this restlessness is as of a Self, a sense of individuality, somehow out of place.

This may sound like some kind of plea for corporate identity, each individual in its place, united for some given purpose. It is no such thing. The places of the spirit I foresee are not graveyards of rural conformity. They are, rather, where people find an identity that is never the same yet is always implicate in the community as a whole. One recalls in this connecion how it was said of mediaeval Europe that a person could live in a village yet partake of Christendom. The difference today is that, whatever today's counterpart of Christendom might be, it is itself containable in the places we inhabit. By the same token, the days of parochialism are surely past. As to what today's 'Christendom' might be, I would not want to surmise. It is sufficient that the religious question is again being asked.

As for the churches themselves in this new countryside, perhaps after all they are the only catalysts we have. We need our history. But, if ever they are to be occupied again, I think their clocks will be left unwound.

# CHAPTER SIX

# Wholeness in Education

# Wholeness
# in Education

## ENVIRONMENTAL EDUCATION IS DYNAMITE

We must ask ourselves whether between 'education', as conventionally understood, and the environment as it should critically be defined, there does not exist a sort of contradiction: that is, for thinking that education has conventionally been concerned with what is actually hostile to our evolving idea of 'the environment'. This is the primary question I must explore—and, in so doing, it is fairly certain we shall find ourselves faced with wide-ranging questions about our way of life itself.

There is a secondary question. It concerns the relationship between education for the environment and research in planning. In this context the function of education is conceived in terms of the transmission of research. Immediately, however, this raises the question of what actually constitutes research in planning: hence, of whether its transmission can be independent of whatsoever it reveals—or whether, perhaps, research is not rather a process of conceptualization, and thus inseparable from communication itself. In effect, this secondary question is an aspect of the first: for both questions bear upon our very idea of reality—and, in themselves, they constitute a challenge to the scientific posture, that urban life somehow exists independently of those who would understand it, merely awaiting discovery.

Now there is no doubt that educational concepts are seriously under question in many parts of the world. The autonomous youth culture of recent years (such that, now, the adult world as often as not follows the fashions of the young) and student attitudes that challenge not just liberal education itself, are testimony to a profound change in the relationships underlying education. Thus, the relations of teacher and taught are under review, and therefrom the view gains ground that education is more about learning than teaching. At bottom, I myself would argue, this turmoil is sustained by the shift of emphasis—enforced, as much as anything else, by children themselves—from education as a preparation for society (but for what society?) to education as a matter of personal growth.

In fact, however, this crucial schism has long existed in western education. The ruling educational ethic of a rationalist culture, to be sure, has been one that sought to be of use to society—hopefully, of course, to a society always moving towards some ideal form. At the same time, however, a minority, or 'progressive,' ethic stressing the child as a child—through the line of Rousseau, Montessori, Homer Lane, A. S. Neill—has continued to exert a curious intellectual power, contrasting strikingly with its tiny numerical strength. Today, however, it is this minority (perhaps because it is being appropriated by the young themselves) that strongly challenges education, conventionally conceived. School itself is even under question, and de-schooling has been given its own rationale. Compulsory education is also being questioned, as it has never been for a hundred years. And, for urban classrooms where the authority of the teacher is notoriously defied, various alternatives to 'school' are being contrived. What these developments are demonstrating, however, is that between these two ethics of education there is as yet no reconciliation in sight. No bridge of discourse has yet been found between an education with an ethic founded on the person and one founded on society—just as, I would contend (for all the efforts of Erikson and Marcuse), no common language has yet been established between Freud and Marx.

Now, whether or not this analysis interests you, you must be beginning to wonder about its bearing upon the question of the environment. Actually, this bearing is superficially not far to seek. Schooling, conventionally conceived, has always been subject-based. Indeed, this has been implicit in the rationalistic structure of education, as being a pursuit essentially of use to society; and, in its turn, such education has fairly reflected Western culture generally, in which the abstractions of science have served as a method to master our hostile world. The environment, conversely, crosses all the boundaries of our subjects. Indeed we invoke it, as an idea, for just such a reason: it is precisely a reaction against, an antidote to, our method of understanding (and hence manipulating) the world by dividing it into its distinct subjects. There is thus on the face of it an affinity between the growing concern for the environment and the (likewise growing) progressive educational ethic, which rejects educational utilitarianism.

This point, however, needs elaboration. It rests, ultimately, upon the idea of given space from which we derive the concept of the environment. Now this idea we have of space is inalienable from the bodies, or things, that inhabit it. Such bodies, however, have each their autonomy in space, which serves to define their interactions, one upon another. Thus, space must also be shared, passively, by bodies not actually in interaction with one another—and this shared space is environmental in kind. In this way, our notion of the environment is integral to the way we seek in our culture to understand reality.

Although it is integral to our understanding, however, the environment is more latent than active in our thinking. Actively, we are concerned with functions: we are concerned, say, with the activity that produces the chimney smoke that incidentally makes the environment for all those not engaged in whatever that function is: or with the house to be lived in, that thereby makes the environment of other people's lives. And each discrete function has its well-established calculus: its language, in terms of which it can rationally be conducted. But the environment, because of the passive part it plays in the system of our understanding—and not being comprehended within any one function—has no such calculus, no such language—and, indeed, doubtfully can acquire one.

Not surprisingly, then, the language of protest has become associated with our growing concern for the environment. The environment has become the cause of the disestablished young. Perhaps inescapably, in these circumstances, the discourse about it is confused, indeed muddled. Precisely because it is not, cannot be, specific, the cause of the environment can be made to seem all things to all people. (The Stockholm World Conference on the Environment may yet founder on this rock; the all-inclusiveness of the environment idea provides many sticks for those minded to beat their foes.) The environment, indeed, can readily be made to stand for the abiding good in a world made wicked by the interested actions of established parties. The language of the environment, therefore, tends to be less distinguished by its logical clarity than by its energy, its passion—indeed, by its repressed passion. Consequently, and particularly in its concern for the environment of the decaying inner city, it tends to be a language less of reform than of a (probably hopeless) acceptance—indeed, a eulogization—of the poverty accompanying that decay.

Yet, for myself, I do not think we should disregard this sometimes incoherent talk. I regard it, rather, as a language seeking to be born. I suggest, in fact, this concern with the environment is the counterpart to disillusion with the fragmented world we have made for ourselves by our rationalistic cast of thought; it is an escape from the characteristic sickness of alienation, the loss of personal identity, which those rationalistic processes have brought upon us. Now, society is a concept we owe to that same cast of thought, and is something we strive to understand, like nature, by dissection into its discrete parts. In the course of this understanding, we take as our social atom the individual, not as a person, but as a player of roles. Hence, in this light, the dichotomy of our educational ethics—of the one founded on the person, the other on society—is but the epitome of a general dialogue of the deaf, as between holistic and scientific thought. Is it too much to propose that until that vacuum of discourse is filled, the development of mankind (or at least of Western mankind) is blocked? And if so, must we not be kindly disposed to the sometimes blind efforts of the environmental discussion to forge an instrument of escape from the prison we have made for ourselves?

At all events, there should be no underrating the force that the discussion of environmental ideas can exert on our traditional educational structures. Authority in our conventional schools is itself subject-based. The teacher's knowledge of his subject—indeed, its mystique—is the key to his status, and hence to much of his authority. When these subject boundaries are crossed, as happens if an environmental approach is introduced into the classroom, the authority of the teachers concerned is put at risk; their relationships with the children need to find a different basis. Either some unifying dynamic must then imbue the school—say, some common social, or even political, purpose—or relationships between staff and children must become personal, rather than authoritarian. All this, at least, seems to have been the observation of researchers into the sociology of education at London University. And yet, that schools must increasingly introduce 'environmental studies'—at least for the growing numbers of children disaffected by school, scholastically understood—is quite apparent.

But, of course, the transformation from one ethic to the other is not proving straightforward. Inevitably no doubt, the conventional ethic has sought to appropriate to itself this dangerous new concept of the environment. Pertinent to this issue there lies an ambiguity inherent in the English word 'appreciation'. It can mean either to like, or to understand— and it carries the suggestion, that to understand is to like. 'Education for environmental appreciation', therefore carries all the connotations of instruction in something to be accepted: in fact, a new subject in the conventional curriculum.

The educational world, in Britain at least, is all too inevitably divided on this issue. In any case, however, examinations in environmental studies, to take their place in the range of all the other subjects of the curriculm, have already been devised. This attempted take-over by the Establishment of what essentially is challenging it, however, no more than parallels the use to which the idea of the environment has been put in planning at large. The notion of an 'environmental area', for instance, first emerged from traffic planning. Such areas were conceived as being free from through traffic, thereby being left to themselves—secluded from disagreeable contact with the world. Naturally, there-fore, the environment has become associated with privilege: with pleasant areas in our cities to be kept uncontaminated by the drawbacks of contemporary life. The Barnsbury district in London has been only the most notorious example of this, where the resurgent middle-class made 'the environment' their justification for diverting all heavy traffic onto their working-class neighbours. Indeed, on the wider scale, it could be said 'the environment' has been appropriated by the middle-classes. It has become a weapon to defend their residential privileges, to keep the spreading town away. Against this, I know, it might be argued that in Britain we have after all designated Environmental Priority Areas in our decaying inner cities, providing certain funds to cheer them up. Indeed, you can see some such Areas in Liverpool, in all their pathos; and you will be able to judge for yourselves from the cosmetics you will note, whether the idea of the environment has not been debased by a certain divorce from its real significance.

For the environment is not, cannot be, just another instrument of our functionally-minded ethos, one to be possessed or benevolently disposed of. It is, rather, the inescapable sum of all those separate functions and of that mind. And the more it is made into a subject like any other, the more will it emerge in some other form and by another name—and the more will those exposed to the tyranny of subjects rebel.

I know I must seem close to saying the environment is something about which we can do nothing—except perhaps to celebrate or decry it (and that would not be negligible). Leaving that point for the moment aside, I think there is indeed a dilemma inherent to environmental studies. Can they in fact be taught? It is said there are now some thirty five teacher training colleges in Britain offering courses in environmental studies. It is also said, however, this is a grandiloquent term for what is actually being done. Whilst I must not pre-judge the matter, it would not be surprising if this were so. It may be, of course, we have here the discipline of geography under another name. But one wonders whether what is intrinsically an anti-subject can be fitted into the structure of schooling—unless, somehow, the meaning of 'school' itself is to change. Certainly, I myself am ignorant of any body of knowledge, as such, that could justify teaching about the environment as a course

I suppose I shall be challenged here, because of the recent great ferment in educational circles over environmental studies. Indeed, at the risk of being parochial, I should cite that in Britain, largely under the aegis of the School's Council (the quasi-official advisory body on the curriculm) examination courses on environmental studies are upon the point of approval. Thus, for 'A' level examinations taken at seventeen or eighteen, essentially in preparation for university, a complex syllabus has been fixed. This syllabus covers such diverse fields as: The Solar System, The Atmosphere and Hydrosphere: The Lithosphere: The Biosphere: Climatic and Edaphic Factors: Pyramids of Numbers: Food Webs: Ecology of Population: Population Control Measures: Ecology of Communities: Man as a Heterotrophic Organism: The Evolution of Man as a Tool-using Rational Creature: Pressures on the Environment (including as sub-sections the Industrial Revolution and the effects of urbanization): Industry and its Environmental Effects—and so on. Likewise, at 'O' level (the lower age-range of secondary education) another syllabus has been prepared, interestingly enough with an entirely rural bias. Now to my mind, all this is simply a conglomeration of subjects, not a subject in itself; it simply amounts to a course in Liberal Studies, with a bias towards the physical sciences. I say this because all these subjects share only the method which in fact divides them. Not all the king's horses nor all the king's professors can put this fragmented Humpty Dumpty together again*. I wonder, do our educationalists realise it is Cartesian method itself that environmental method is challenging.

I mustn't be dogmatic. There may yet be a saving grace in all this resurgent academicism. In the marking of these English examinations a predominance is to be given to teachers' assessments of course work, and only a minority to marks of examination papers as such. As for world-wide interest in the development of environmental studies, something can be gleaned from a UNESCO enquiry published in 1968—and yet, again, I cannot hide my disquiet that this is

---

* English Nursery Rhyme:
  Humpty Dumpty sat on a wall,
  Humpty Dumpty had a great fall.
  All the King's horses and all the King's men
  Couldn't put Humpty together again.

a collection of international bromides. I must further recognize that in the United States an Environmental Education Act was passed in 1970, providing $45m over three years for the development of environmental education—but by now my scepticism will not surprise you, if I prefer to wait and see whether this money can produce any proportionate results.

Does this then mean that the environment is indeed something about which nothing can be done?—because, logically, anything one does about it must itself in turn produce environmental effects? For example, to clean up the environment of the North West of England—to plant up the slag heaps, clean the air, de-contaminate the rivers, eradicate the urban decay—would not such purposeful activities be quite practicable? Happily, yes! But is this not because the North West has become (by its very degeneration) recognizable as a thing in itself, a thing—in fact, a region—of which we can treat directly? And if we do treat of this 'environment' which is in fact a region, shall we not hopefully be causing it to disappear—leaving as a result of our efforts the amorphous environment, indistinguishable from England at large?

The sense of this example is to suggest that actually we call 'the environment' in aid when we identify problems to which our normal, functional calculus is not adapted. This points, I think, to what is really being thrown up by the current concern for questions of the environment. This concern is indicating that there are various forms of life not tractable to measurement, or to some externally applied rule. Here, of course, we begin to touch upon the nature of research, as it affects planning. For these forms I have in mind are many of them urban in kind, or to do with human settlements: cities, towns, villages, regions. And, such is the authority of our climate of rationalistic thought, if forms seem to exist for which no measure can be found, we are prone to banish them to the amorphous realm of 'the environment'. In that realm, the actual problems of those forms–for example, the whole threat to our established urban order, of cities and towns, from the mobility now at Everyman's command—can be disregarded: or, more likely, under the protection of the 'environment' the established order can offer a privileged defence against this threat. What we call the problems of the environment, in fact, are in large part the problems of facing up to a new urban order, from which quite naturally we would rather avert our minds.

Our minds, however, would the less readily be averted from those problems if simultaneously we could bring ourselves to recognize there are forms of life to which our idolatry of measurement is indeed not applicable—but which yet remain veritable forms. These forms, I suggest, are actually articulated by the continuing discourse we hold about them—just as they are confirmed by the possibility of any such discourse being held. Nowadays, for instance, it is increasingly difficult to discourse about 'the city'; to discourse about the region, however, comes ever more easily. To me, this cannot but suggest that research itself is a matter of such discourse, of such articulation of urban forms. That is to say, research is a matter of illumination of the forms by which we seek to understand one another. It is not a matter of ascertaining some reality independent of such communication.

The theoretical justification for this view, of course, lies in the fact of language. This fact determines that those who would investigate the workings of society are constrained by the terms within which those workings themselves are conducted. Obversely, only an illumination of those terms can provide a meaningful comment upon what is being investigated. Of course, this view of research is repungant to the puristic social scientist. He would hold that, as mass is a property of natural objects, so is value the property of social objects—and so he would contend that theoretically we can determine the behaviour of all social phenomena. It is to this contention, of course, we owe the late arrival of cost-benefit analysis onto the scene of urban research; it constitutes an attempt to measure in its own right each discrete component of some common urban field, setting the form aside. The debacle of the Roskill inquiry into the Third London Airport, however, has already and probably fatally discredited that attempt to impute monetary measurements to situations, and across boundaries, for which those measurements were never devised. A little knowledge of linguistic philosophy might have saved the Roskill Commission a deal of hurt pride—just as its application to the study of economics itself is now long overdue.

Now, if this view of the necessary character of urban research be sound, it carries implications for my theme. In the first instance, it restores to primacy the qualities of human judgement, in place of the presumed certainties of research into some independent reality. (You could cite this, if you wished, as part of the ongoing counter-Copernican revolution: the restoration of Man to the centre of the universe.) But research thus conceived does not have findings that can be transmitted as received knowledge, as conventional schooling would require. Rather, only an involvement in the discourse can give access to the research. Education too, therefore, if it is to benefit from research and if that research is to be implemented in the learning process, must also partake of the discourse.

The implication of this, it seems to me, is that environmental education at least must be concerned neither with teaching nor learning. If it is to be anything at all, it must be concerned with doing. That is to say, to understand the environment one must be involved in actualities. Children therefore must partake in the controversies—whether about polluted streams, the impact of motorways, the siting of reservoirs; they must do the surveys and evaluate the results—that is, if we want the environment to enter into their education. What this might do to our schools is a different question—and what will happen to them if we do not do it is another question again.

I am aware that in saying this I have used the term 'environment' in the very sense I have myself questioned. But in the last analysis I would not want to quibble over this. If we talk about the environment when really we should be discussing newly-emerging urban forms, nevertheless any such discussion makes quite new demands upon our comprehension. They both require us to cross the technical boundaries that conventionally structure so much discourse. And this, in effect, means the forging of some new language.

If I predict the necessity for this new language, I am nevertheless not under an obligation to you to invent it before your eyes. Of this very necessity, however, I have no doubt. Our concern over the environment, as I have tried to show, is a symptom of this necessity, and I do not believe it is a passing phase. The questioning is deep and spreading about the alienating processes of our technological culture. Marx made the gigantic attempt to bring Natural Man and society together, and his failure leaves us with a yet more gigantic question about Western culture. The pending upheaval in the professions both of planning and of teaching is perhaps the least of changes in store.

Now, I have already suggested that doing, rather than teaching or learning, is how in principle we shall form a new language about the environment. If, however, beyond this I am asked how this language might evolve, I would hazard it must come with a new concept of space—not as given, but as continuously created. I say this, not because I harbour some scientific notion of the physical universe, but because in these terms I could understand how the idea of a person and the idea of society—of what is internal and what is environmental—could be subsumed in the logic of one discourse. Such a world, not so much divided up, but continuously being made, would be one to which mechanistic thought was foreign. It would therefore be immeasurably different from our own. But of course, I am starting to chase shadows. I must content myself by concluding in suitably old-fashioned terms with my view, that environmental education is dynamite.

# THE PULSE OF UNCERTAINTY

School is the institutionalized epitome of dualism. After all, dualism is how we make sense of our lives: mind and body, the self and the World, observer and observed, subject and object, etc. Dualism indeed is endemic in language—and we are encaged in language. Knowledge, or what in the West we take to be 'knowledge', comes from this dualism; and through it we have mastered the natural world (or think we have). Schools, then, are places where we manipulate children as we manipulate the world, and where we impose knowledge upon them.

It is against this prologue that one must view the collapse of the education system, which we are seeing almost before our eyes. For what we are witnessing is much more than a mechanical breakdown in a system—which is something that prescriptions such as Tertiary Colleges, or Middle Schools, or Sixth Form Colleges, might put right. Rather, our dualistic way of understanding, of making sense of life, is itself in question, and this is but manifested in the dissatisfaction with our schools. In everyday terms, schools are failing to provide the meal ticket for the young whom we put in their charge: not, however, because their teaching has failed, but because the meals are no longer there.

The sadness of this is that, after all, schools are in spirit more real than the world itself. In schools, knowledge is still merely knowledge, and curiosity still curiosity; it is not yet the instrument of power over Nature (including other men) it becomes in life. There is still a passage—albeit its rites are debased—from childhood to the adult state when the child leaves school for the 'outside world;' and, especially in some urban areas, schools still have a very necessary sheltering function. Yet, after all, the 'knowledge' in question is ultimately the knowledge society recognizes as such, and which can be made to serve it. In practice, then, schools are not other than the world itself, and are held on its leash and so brought to heel.

In speaking here of 'schools' one is, of course, thinking of orthodoxy. There are other kinds of schools, generally called 'progressive'. Their light has waned since the last war, simultaneously with the tremendous growth in popular, or State, education. No doubt, great hopes were pinned upon the latter, hopes some of which progressive education had previously carried, of serving some other purpose than orthodox schooling—and particularly other than its pro-consular pretensions. The new orthodoxy, however, was but social engineering writ large, not a substitute for progressive education at all—and several decades have been wasted in this confusion. For progressive education, classically understood, is not about knowledge but, rather, about the knower: about the person as a person, the child as a child, and their development as such.

Here we have the very nub of dualism. To explain:- the progenitor of progressive education in our time was Rousseau, the father of the Romantic Movement and the conceiver of 'Natural Man'. To the (then) young intellectuals of the post-war orthodoxy in education—the Comprehensive School movement—Rousseau was, if not unheard of, almost a figure of fun. None the less, it is worth savouring some of the flavour of his *Emile*, if only because it is still more truly radical than anything dreamed of by the post war theorists. For instance:

Childhood is the sleep of reason.

Childhood has its own ways of seeing, thinking, and feeling. *[This is where child psychology, as we know it, began.]*

They are always looking for the man in the child, without considering what he is before he becomes a man.

What a poor sort of foresight to make a child wretched in the present with the more or less doubtful hope of making him happy at some future day.

Every stage, every station in life has a perfection of its own.

Reading is the curse of childhood . . . When I thus get rid of children's lessons I get rid of the chief cause of their sorrow.

Work or play are all one to him, his games are his work, he knows no difference.

You must make your choice between the man and the citizen, you cannot train both.

Let him know nothing because you have told him, but because he has learnt it himself.

When he fancies himself as a workman, he is becoming a philosopher.

Alas! all that richness went out of the window when the new social engineering moved in. The content of education became the academic curriculum, rather, with its division of knowledge into 'subjects'—specialisms, for taming the world—grouped around its Sixth Form in any school large enough economically to justify cultivation of the whole arid spectrum. Given this premise of knowledge, the grammar school tail has wagged the comprehensive school dog and brought the contradictions of education itself to a head. For romanticism was, as a reaction against materialism (one at least suited to its times), an expression of the perennial dualism of our civilization. It asserted the autonomy of the person—in practice, the Artist—over against the world. Rousseau thus countered Descartes, much as God and Caesar had formerly outfaced each other.

Our dualism of mind and body, then, has its most pregnant—even religious—manifestation in that distinction of which each of us is surely aware: the distinction between ourselves and the universe we inhabit. Language, after all, virtually imposes this distinction upon us by its subject-object relationships, and, in so doing, is the predicate of God, whereby that division is to be reconciled under Providence. ('God would not deceive us,' said Descartes of the gap his logic posited between the Self and that about which it thought.) Since education is about the knowledge we have of the world, this profound aspect of our human condition is bound to be reflected in it. In truth, not only Rousseau, but nearly all the philosophers of education, both before and since him, have stressed the individuality of the child—whilst, just as consistently, the practitioners in the schools have served the world.

Yet the fact is that progressive and orthodox education exist in a symbiotic relationship. That is why progressive education was, characteristically, so reactive against orthodoxy. And it is why, nowadays, the downfall of mass education has not been accompanied by the triumph of the progressive minority. Both are outworn. The malady goes deeper than education itself.

Now let it be clear, this is not the start of any contention on my part that we must escape from dualism. Indeed, the root of the trouble might be diagnosed as the belief of either party to our dualistic life—those who serve God, or those who serve Caesar: those who would abjure, or those who would master, the world—that theirs is the sole course to follow. This, alas! is as true as those, following in the wake of John Dewey, who believed in 'learning by doing,' as of those who teach reflective knowledge from books. Learning by doing, for sure, provides a very real kind of knowledge: inner knowledge, comparable perhaps to the gnosticism of old, and like it it focuses upon the doer, upon he who has this knowledge (upon Rousseau's workman who is becoming a philosopher). Yet we must beware of escaping from the servitude of pedagogues to that of materialists. 'Doing,' by taking part in the world's business, is not necessarily educative. The fact is, so long as we have language, we cannot actually escape from dualism.

What we can do, rather, is to be aware of our condition. Now, to be aware of our condition is to recognize that when we are concerned with the person we cannot know about the world, and when we learn about the world we cannot know about the person. Life, in other words is a kind of pulse: the pulse of uncertainty. Conceived as such, it is not susceptible to the monistic passion to utopianize the world, to remake the Garden of Eden. It is mankind's very command of speech that makes impossible this sort of wholeness. (One wonders, is monism what we call 'the emotions'? It is significant that a Buddhist will speak rather of 'non-dualism' than of 'holism.') Rather, the pulse of life calls for certain forms to be observed if any meaning is to be found in it. In fact, the accusation that lies against the quantitative knowledge by which our schools have become dominated—just as our civilization is dominated—is that it has brought us to a formless Age, a way of life that is fragmented and meaningless. No wonder 'Things fall apart, the centre cannot hold', or that the authority of the teacher's certitudes is falling into contempt!

Schools, in this scenario, should not really be necessary. As it is, however, they are an admission of society's failure: they are the surrogates of community. We do not have a society in which schools could be dispensed with, because we have lost (or all but lost) the communities a child would need in order for the knowledge he acquires to be made meaningful. (Conversely, we have a growing store of meaningless knowledge.) Interestingly, Rousseau chose

Emile from an aristocratic family, rather than a child of the lower orders, because his highly artificial background made Emile more in need of saving as a person. The lower classes, Rousseau thought, were closer to a natural life. Maybe! but when we have a whole world of bourgeois values, as now, how shall we learn from Nature?

That world does not any more exist in which to be a person is also compatible with, say, altruism. To be a 'person', today, is almost tantamount to being egocentric. Conversely, to not be selfish in a materialistic society is nearly suicidal: to give of 'oneself' in a world of quantitative values stretches credulity. This rot has attacked the roots of progressive education also. What it means, surely, if paradoxically, is that we are entering one of those phases in history where whatsoever is meaningful has to be recreated. Thus schools, if they are to have any validity, should perhaps set themselves to become models for the world.

This is not as far-fetched as it might have sounded even a few years ago. With the world no longer available to young people on leaving school—and the ten-year old son of one of my friends said to him the other day, 'Daddy, what shall I do when I'm unemployed?'—schools are having to contrive a world of their own for young people: a world in which the Manpower Services Commission, rather than the Department of Education, is having an increasing influence upon what passes for 'education'. At all events, the opportunity is there for the taking, of schools becoming more real than the 'real' world: of turning themselves into places where qualitative values hold sway, where inner as well as outer knowledge is cultivated, where wealth is as much environmental as private or discrete, where Nature is lived with rather than mastered: perhaps, most fundamentally, a world not obsessed with the Self and its salvation, which makes of the world its chattel. After all, the monasteries achieved something like this at a moment of history somewhat comparable to the present.

To draw this analogy, however, is almost as much as to admit how undesirable, even if practicable, it would be for our schools to make this transformation on their own. To be a model is not to be the thing itself. The hope should rather be that schools might be the catalysts of change: of change, that is, in their surrounding communities—or what should become their surrounding communities—such that between school and community there would come to be no perceptible difference. (At least, the curriculum might then be determined by the community, rather than the community becoming the mere residue, as now, the 'catchment area,' of subject functions.) But of course, this presumes huge social changes, and the reversal of trends towards the large and impersonal in scale going back over more than two hundred years.

Yet it is not impossible. Between the hierarchical society of orthodox education and the anarchical society (so unnerving to some) of the true progressive school—in which Martin Buber's 'I—Thou' word necessarily obtains, in all its forlorn nobility—there must surely be another course. It is one that can only be made possible, however, in a community whose members themselves take responsibility for its children. For where this happens knowledge will have meaning and children will no more be manipulated than the community would manipulate itself. (Perhaps the Kibbutz would repay more study?) The duality of our life would be inescapably present in such circumstances: the child would both grow as a child, for he would be known personally by his teachers, and he would acquire knowledge of the world. Pace Rousseau, he would become both man and citizen. But neither component would be enshrined in a principle, or institutionalized, to the exclusion of the other. The community, if it is to have any reality, would not allow this. It is not, in the end, education that must change society, but society education, because education has no separate existence.